Contents

Introductory activities

Part 1: Activities exploring interconnectedness

Part 2: Activities exploring fairness

Part 3: Activities exploring sustainability

Global Learning and Special Educational Needs

Working with local producers and craftspeople

Acknowledgements

The following publications from CDEC are required as an essential part of many of the activities within this handbook:

Meet Zogg: an alien arrives on earth, and makes friends with Boy and Mouse. Together they explore earth and its people, places and customs. A beautifully illustrated big book that focuses on global citizenship; themes include waste, recycling and sustainable development, respecting diversity and games around the world.

Thea Discovers Chocolate: an imaginative big storybook featuring Thea, a teddy bear who leads children through a journey of exploring Fairtrade, which takes her from Grandma's farm all the way to a cocoa farm in Belize.

Lily's Picnic: Lily meets new friends in her neighbourhood, including a beekeeper, baker, and basket maker, who help her hold a delicious picnic all using locally produced food. Introduces children to the themes of local interdependence, sustainability, and community.

All three books are available from CDEC, contact: office@cdec.org.uk

 A project funded by the European Union and led in England by CDEC.

How to use this handbook

The activities in this handbook have been developed by teachers and practitioners in schools and nurseries in Bulgaria, Cyprus, Poland and the UK as part of the World from our Doorstep project. Many take inspiration from, or have been adapted from, activities developed alongside the Meet Zogg and Thea Discovers Chocolate story books (produced by Cumbria Development Education Centre). All are written with the 3 – 8 year old age range in mind, some are more suitable for younger children and some for older children. Most of the activities included are adaptable to reflect the needs of the age range you are working with.

The handbook is designed so you can work through it from start to finish, or use the sections in any order. Whichever you do, the introductory pages are here to help you get the messages right, and put your global education work in context, as well as to provide advice, ideas and resources.

- Introductory activities have an orange background
- Part 1 – Activities exploring interconnectedness have a green background
- Part 2 – Activities exploring fairness have a red background
- Part 3 – Activities exploring sustainability have a blue background

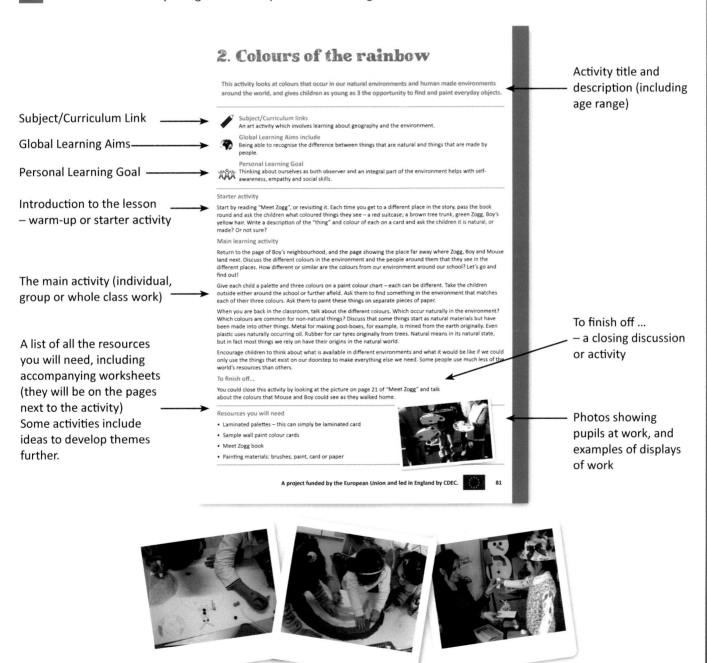

Activity title and description (including age range)

Subject/Curriculum Link

Global Learning Aims

Personal Learning Goal

Introduction to the lesson – warm-up or starter activity

The main activity (individual, group or whole class work)

A list of all the resources you will need, including accompanying worksheets (they will be on the pages next to the activity) Some activities include ideas to develop themes further.

To finish off ... – a closing discussion or activity

Photos showing pupils at work, and examples of displays of work

Introduction

Our children are growing up in an increasingly complex and global world, in which their lives are connected to people and places at the click of a button, or by the purchase of a chocolate bar. The skills and understanding needed to be a "global citizen" are crucial for children as never before. Research in the UK found a very high level of public support for the idea that all members of society should have the opportunity to learn about global issues, with almost nine in ten (86%) of the British public agreeing that global learning in school is crucial if these issues are to be tackled in future.

But engaging young children in learning about these challenging and complex issues can be difficult and daunting. "The World from our Doorstep" is an approach to global learning aimed at teachers and practitioners working with younger children (aged 3—8). Schools from the UK, Bulgaria, Cyprus and Poland have worked together to explore what complex global themes – such as interdependence, fairness, and sustainability – mean for younger children, and how they can be incorporated into teaching and learning in ways that are fun, engaging, relevant and meaningful. This handbook contains a range of activities and lesson ideas that have been tried and tested with younger children.

We have been working with pre-school practitioners, infant teachers, teaching assistants and other adult helpers, to build their confidence and expertise so that they can incorporate challenging and stimulating global learning into their day to day work with young children.

Why is this resource needed?

Young children are at a crucially formative stage when their interests, values and attitudes, and the way they think of themselves and relate with others – key characteristics that will determine how they think and act in later life – are germinated and grown. They also have a natural curiosity and concern for fairness, a core concept in global learning. The World from our Doorstep approach creates global learning opportunities for younger children which create the conditions for them to think, act, and learn differently, giving them the opportunity to develop global–mindedness, and begin to understand that their lives are connected to people and places far beyond their local context.

Pre-school and infant practitioners are not specifically trained in subject areas and may feel less confident in teaching about global issues. The World from our Doorstep activities make it very easy for teachers to realize that global learning starts locally; it's about personal development and self-identity, and how we relate to our local community and environment, just as much as it's about thinking about other countries and the way we are connected with other people and places.

Teachers of young children have many opportunities to support children's learning on global issues. Early Years curricula are generally rich in thematic working, providing flexibility for practitioners to link project themes to everyday teaching. In the UK, the Early Years Foundation Stage curriculum (2014) includes an area of learning 'knowledge and understanding of the world' but we find that practitioners tend to focus only on the world around them, whereas we want to extend this reach to introduce global understanding.

Despite the curriculum opportunities there is a lack of age-appropriate materials for introducing the concepts of global awareness with this age group, so there is a huge opportunity for further developing global learning through new stories and games. This Practitioner's handbook is designed to be an easy-to-use approach to establishing the foundations of global learning in your work with younger children.

"Why do kindergartens offer more for moving towards a more sustainable world than many of our universities? Kindergartens ideally are places where young children live and learn, explore boundaries, in a safe and transparent world without hidden agendas. Kindergartens are places where conflict emerges every day and is used as a 'teachable' moment. Kindergartens today often are multi-cultural places where children with different backgrounds come together and get to know each other as they are, not as they are portrayed by others. Kindergartens are also places where different generations meet and interact (children, parents, grandparents). They are often located in the heart of the community. There are no dumb questions in kindergarten and there's always time for questions and questioning. The life-world of the child forms the starting point for learning, not a disciplinary problem. There is room for exploration, discovery and multiple ways of expressing oneself. It's a place filled with energy. And there are some basic rules, principles, and skills needed to function in an organic whole." Kindergartens as a learning context for ESD (Finnish UNESCO Series on ESD. Shaping the Education of Tomorrow: 2012 Report on the UN Decade of Education http://www.desd.org/UNESCO%20report.pdf)

*For more information see *The Impact of Global Learning on Public Attitudes and Behaviours towards International Development and Sustainability* (2010) by Think Global (formerly DEA).

 A project funded by the European Union and led in England by CDEC.

Subject areas/ Curriculum links

PAINTING THE WORLD

Teachers in the UK, Bulgaria, Poland and Cyprus have used these resources in a wide range of subject areas in class, as part of whole school or topic work, or during off-site activities. In England primary schools are currently working with the introduction of the Primary Curriculum, while teachers of younger children will be working within the Early Years Framework. Where an activity lends itself well to a particular curriculum/ subject area we mention it in the activity description – otherwise teachers will be able to adapt and relate the activities to their own needs.

In England, practitioners working with children under five will be using the Early Years Framework which:

- Sets the standards that all early years providers must meet to ensure that children learn and develop well

- Ensures children are kept healthy and safe

- Ensures that children have the knowledge and skills they need to start school

Find a link to it here: **https://www.gov.uk/government/publications/early-years-foundation-stage-framework-2**

The page hosting all the subject area curricula for England Primary schools can be found here:

https://www.gov.uk/government/publications/national-curriculum-in-england-primary-curriculum

We also point you to the Global Learning Programme which has further information on incorporating global learning into the primary curriculum:

http://globaldimension.org.uk/glp

Think Global's Global Dimension website has a three page briefing on the global dimension in the new primary curriculum which you can download for free from here.

http://globaldimension.org.uk/news/item/19611 with links to plenty of other subject related resources.

Another useful place for support in linking to particular curriculum areas can be found with the relevant association for that subject. Many have free downloads, tables summarizing links to the curriculum and other support. Some relevant links:

Geographical Association: http://www.geography.org.uk/news/2014nationalcurriculum/primarynccontent/

Physical, Social, Health and Economic Education Association: https://www.pshe-association.org.uk/content.aspx?CategoryID=1053

Association for Physical Education: http://www.afpe.org.uk/advice-on-new-national-curriculum/new-national-curriculum

Association for Science Education: http://www.ase.org.uk/curriculum/

National Association for the Teaching of English: www.nate.org.uk

Association of Teachers of Mathematics: http://www.atm.org.uk/Home

You'll also find a Times Educational Supplement guide to the new National Curriculum here:

http://info.tes.co.uk/free-teaching-guides/changes-to-the-national-curriculum/

Being a Global Teacher

Embedding a global perspective into the learning environment is not all about countries and themes, and doing specific "global" activities. It is more about how the world is reflected and represented in the everyday routine and about emphasising similarities across the world, rather than differences.

Each activity within the handbook comes with its own suggestions for things to do, questions to ask and things to avoid. Here are some general tips:

Always try to...

✓ Stress whereabouts in the world any stories or examples within the activities come from, and that similar events could take place anywhere.

✓ Focus on the similarities between the children's lives and the lives of other children described in the activities or associated stories.

✓ Always seek to challenge stereotypes and provide a range of images and examples.

✓ Celebrate what is unique and special about people everywhere.

Try not to...

✗ Generalise about a whole country or continent from the examples within the activities or accompanying resources. All countries are made up of contrasts: rich/poor, urban/rural, traditional/contemporary.

✗ Be afraid to say when you don't know something – global education is about learning how to find things out together.

✗ Treat the natural world as something "out there", remember that people, along with all living and non-living things, are integral and connected parts of what makes up the planet.

The handbook is intended to enable children and those working with them to look at the world and the people in it with respect and without prejudice. It lays a foundation for children to experience the world from a position of confidence in their own identity, and the belief that they can and will influence the world around them. It also provides a platform for parents and carers to find out more, learning alongside their children.

The activities in this handbook are based on a particular set of methodologies: Philosophy for Children, experiential learning, participatory and child-led learning, and dialogic learning. These approaches are intended to move away from the typical understanding of learning, in which the teacher is the expert and it is his/her role to impart objective knowledge to their pupils. Global learning approaches require children to learn – through experience – that there often isn't a right or wrong answer to some big and complex problems. It is through critical thinking, listening, dialogue, and recognizing that there can be multiple and relative perspectives that children learn how to understand a range of different issues. The teacher becomes "the guide on the side" rather than "the sage on the stage". This can sometimes feel uncomfortable...but ultimately you will see the results in terms of children's engagement, empowerment, confidence, and the depth of their learning and relationships with others.

> **"I think we should all try much harder to get on with each other because it makes us smile more."**
>
> **(Child in Cumbria, UK)**

> **"Children can enrich their knowledge and broaden their horizons. They learn to think beyond the narrow confines of their environment and express concerns that connect globally."**
>
> **(Eftychia Nikolau, Teacher, Kolossiou 1 Nursery School, Cyprus)**

  A project funded by the European Union and led in England by CDEC.

Global Learning Aims

During the project, global learning professionals and teachers in each of the partner countries identified key global learning aims – things that our next generation of global citizens need to learn to equip them to take action for change and make the world a better place. The activities in this handbook are designed to help develop these key elements of knowledge and understanding, values and attitudes, and behaviours and skills. They are summarised below, with examples of activities that support that element listed by title.

We have not differentiated between aims for the early years ages and the Key Stage 1 age group (relevant for England) as the basic concept behind the aims are the same. The level at which children achieve against that aim will depend on the individual class and teacher; the context and how they develop the activities; and what direction the discussion takes

Knowledge and understanding:

Children will be able to...	Activities that support this
1. Express their understanding of a story or activity in relation to their own experiences	Welcoming Zogg to our school Journey with Zogg or Thea
2. Express awareness of others, and similarities and difference in relation to themselves	Community connections Stacking hands
3. Begin to understand how their actions affect others, and consider what might happen if they acted differently	Get creative with Zogg Planet Earth – learning from Zargot
4. Understand that some of the food they eat comes from their own country, and some from elsewhere, and the way it is grown, produced and transported has an impact on people and the planet	Where does food come from? What's for breakfast today?
5. Begin to have a sense of their connections with the wider world, and between other people and places	Journey with Zogg or Thea Name game
6. Know what is fair and unfair personally, and that we don't all have access to the same things	Fruitcake frenzy Puzzle time
7. Recognise the difference between things that are natural, and things that are made by people	Colours of the rainbow Mapsticks
8. Understand that we are all part of the environment and our actions have an impact on it	Exploring my neighbourhood with Zogg Gifts from the sea
9. Understand that there are many different environments on earth and we rely on and use lots of natural resources from them, and we need to look after them	Mapsticks Gifts from the sea
10. Understand the basic principles of Fairtrade and other aspects of food production that have an impact on people and the environment	What's Fairtrade? Who made your chocolate

Values and attitudes

Children will show/develop...	Activities that support this
1. Concern for, empathy with and sensitivity to others, locally and globally	Questions for new friends Community connections
2. Positive attitudes towards difference and diversity	Faces of the world I am special
3. A sense of connection with their immediate environment (e.g. the air we breathe, water we drink, food we eat)	Mapsticks Sustainable table
4. Understand that other people being happy and healthy can make the world a nicer place to be for everyone	What's Fairtrade? What's for breakfast?
5. Understand that by sharing and working together, more can be accomplished and things can be more enjoyable	Planet Earth – learning from Zargot Zogg's house
6. A desire to take action and make choices that are good for people and the environment	What's Fairtrade? Planet earth – learning from Zargot
7. A sense of fair play and a willingness to speak out and take action if they think a behaviour is wrong or unfair	That's not fair! Fairtrade market
8. An appreciation of and a desire to look after their own local environment	Exploring my neighbourhood Mapsticks
9. A sense of wonder and curiosity	Gifts from the sea Faces of the world
10. Concern for the global environment and a willingness to care for it	New from old Gifts from the sea

 A project funded by the European Union and led in England by CDEC.

Behaviour and skills

Children will be able to…	Activities that support this
1. Start to take care of things, animate and inanimate	Welcoming Zogg to our school Gifts from the sea
2. Ask questions and listen to others	Journey with Zogg or Thea Questions for new friends
3. Help and show care for others	Cooperative drawing Welcoming Zogg…
4. Share and discuss their ideas with others and begin to justify their opinions	Questions for new friends Sustainable table
5. Respect that people (including themselves) have different cultures	Kim's game Faces of the world
6. Make links between their lives and the lives of others	Faces of the world Breads from around the world
7. Develop cooperation skills, sharing and taking turns as well as collaboration over tasks	Many hands make light work! Fairtrade farmers
8. Begin to identify unfairness and take appropriate action	That's not fair! Who made your chocolate?
9. Communicate how they feel to peers, parents and other adults and clearly express their point of view	Community connections Sustainable table
10. Get involved in sustainable actions in the classroom and at home, e.g. recycling, conserving energy	Planet earth – learning from Zargot Zogg's house

A project funded by the European Union and led in England by CDEC.

Personal Learning Goals

On each activity you will see at least one personal learning goal identified by the teachers who developed that activity. In England there is a framework of Social and Emotional Aspects of Learning, and teachers in England may find it useful to be able to map the activity against those aspects.

As these lessons are developed around creative, participatory, and collaborative methodology, including Philosophy for Children they lessons naturally build a sense of community, offer some form of stimulus and will encourage questioning from children. Clearly, any lesson based on this kind of methodology provides a sound basis for work involving the social and emotional aspects of learning. Children's self-awareness increases, they learn to recognise feelings of their own and of others, and develop empathy and social skills during an enquiry. As the methodology is collaborative and child centred they are also motivated about their own learning.

Self awareness	Children have some understanding of themselves children take responsibility for their own actions
	Children know that feelings, thoughts and behaviors are linked children accept themselves for what and who they are
Managing feelings	Children manage how they express their feelings and can manage the way they are feeling
	Children can reflect and review on experiences to change the way they feel children can adapt the way they express feelings to suit particular situations
Motivation	Children can set goals and plan to meet them children can consider the consequences for others
	Children can put long term plans into achievable steps
	Children can evaluate their own learning and use this to improve in the future
Empathy	Children can understand the feelings of others children understand other peoples points of view
	Children value and respect the thoughts, feelings, values and beliefs of others children can offer support to others
Social skills	Children know that they belong to a community and are valued children can cooperate and achieve a shared outcome
	Children can make wise choices
	Children can solve problems in a logical manner

Information taken from Key document: Excellence and Enjoyment: Social and Emotional Aspects of Learning (SEAL), 05-2005, DfESW 1378-2005 G.

Below you will find a table indicating which of the activities in this handbook develop these aspects of social and emotional learning.

	Social and Emotional Aspect of Learning:	Self Awareness	Managing Feelings	Motivation	Empathy	Social Skills
	General/Introductory Activities					
1.	Name game	✓				✓
2.	Questions for new friends	✓	✓		✓	✓
3.	Cooperative drawing				✓	✓
4.	Welcoming Zogg to our school	✓			✓	✓
5.	I am special	✓	✓			✓
6.	Stacking hands	✓				✓
7.	Exploring my neighbourhood with Zogg	✓				✓
8.	Journey with Zogg or Thea		✓		✓	✓

A project funded by the European Union and led in England by CDEC.

	Interconnectedness					
1.	Community connections	✓				✓
2.	Get creative with Zogg			✓	✓	✓
3.	Faces of the world	✓	✓			✓
4.	Kim's game – what's missing?	✓			✓	
5.	Where does food come from?				✓	
6.	Breads from around the world	✓			✓	
7.	What's for breakfast today?	✓			✓	✓
8.	Many hands make light work			✓		✓
	Fairness					
1.	Puzzle time		✓		✓	
2.	That's not fair	✓			✓	✓
3.	What's Fairtrade?		✓	✓		✓
4.	Who made your chocolate?		✓	✓	✓	✓
5.	Fairtrade farmers			✓	✓	✓
6.	Fairtrade market			✓		✓
	Sustainability					
1.	Appreciating the world	✓				✓
2.	Colours of the rainbow	✓				✓
3.	Fruitcake frenzy	✓	✓		✓	✓
4.	Mapsticks	✓				✓
5.	Gifts from the sea	✓	✓		✓	✓
6.	Zogg's spaceship			✓		✓
7.	Zogg's house	✓	✓		✓	✓
8.	Sustainable table	✓			✓	✓
9.	Planet earth – learning from Zargot!					✓

Introduction to Philosophy for Children

> **"Philosophy can be used to improve teaching and learning, for the lasting benefit of individuals and communities."**
> SAPERE (Society for Advancing Philosophical Enquiry and Reflection in Education)

Philosophy for Children is an important methodology, and central to global education. It is a way of learning and teaching where children become more thoughtful and reflective and go beyond information to seek understanding. Children learn how to participate in meaningful discussions, where their ideas and those of others are valued and listened to. Children ask and discuss philosophical questions in a structured context. A distinctive advantage of P4C, and one which makes it particularly appropriate for global education, is that it gives children an opportunity to consider issues that they would usually be considered "too young" to think about.

What follows is a brief outline of a basic P4C session.

Community building activity (5–15 mins)

Sessions start with a community building activity.

Stimulus (15–30 mins)

This can be a story, case study, photograph, artefact or anything else that will engage the children in philosophical questioning.

Thinking as individuals, discussion in pairs (5 mins)

The pupils are asked to take 30 seconds to think individually about what the stimulus made them think and feel – which might lead them to think of a question they would like to ask. You might ask them to close their eyes. They should then turn to the person next to them and swap their initial thoughts – for about 2 – 3 minutes. This should be a noisy time!

It is important to give pupils time to think as individuals, before they hear from others. Speaking in pairs gives even the quietest pupil the chance to express their thoughts.

Question setting in groups (5 mins)

Pupils are then asked to form groups (say of 4). The teacher should ensure that there is a competent writer in each group. In their groups, they discuss and agree on a question arising from the stimulus that the whole group (class) might discuss together. It is to be a philosophical question – one that is interesting and will lead to deep thinking (and perhaps other questions). Over time (and with additional activities) pupils learn what is a philosophical question (as opposed to a closed question or one that requires factual research).

Voting for one question (5 mins)

Each group is asked to read out their question and to clarify it where needed. Pupils (as individuals) now have to vote for one question. Some dialogue can take place – pupils can be asked to volunteer reasons for their choices – differing views (with reasons) can be sought. Sometimes similar questions can be merged (with agreement). If there is a tie (or almost a tie), pupils can "sell" their favoured question and see if others will vote for it. One question is chosen. There are lots of ways of voting.

Dialogue (30 mins)

Everyone sits in a circle. To start the dialogue, the chosen question is read out and the group that wrote it is asked to provide some of the thinking behind it. Then the job of the facilitator is to encourage all the pupils to contribute thoughts (voluntarily) and seek other ways of looking at the issues, probing for reasons and seeking meaning. Thinking can be stimulated by the development of "effective questions". Some of these are provided at the end of this section. Sometimes an interim summary

  A project funded by the European Union and led in England by CDEC.

of the dialogue will be useful (and, of course, a summary is useful at the end, with a reflection on how far the question has been answered). A facilitator will try to anticipate where the stimulus might lead, but is also flexible as it might lead into unanticipated areas.

Reflection/debrief (5 mins)

There are many debrief techniques. For example, each pupil is encouraged to give a few words about their impressions of the dialogue – perhaps for example something that surprised them, or they learned, or if they changed their mind about something during the session. If struggling, they can say "pass".

The pupils and facilitator might discuss concepts that need further exploration, perhaps during the following session. Any concepts, ideas or questions should be 'stored' for follow-up work by writing them down and putting them on the wall as part of a display. This will help keep the questions fresh in the mind and will allow other thoughts and ideas to flow and be discussed outside of the philosophy session.

P4C– Questions to aid facilitation

Clarifying

What reasons do you have for saying that?

What do you mean by that?

Can you explain more about that? Have you an example of that?

What makes you so sure of that? Probing the superficial

Why do you think that? What is the cause of that? What makes you say that? Why...why...why...?

Seeking Evidence

How do you know that? What makes you say that? What is your evidence?

What are your reasons? What makes you so sure?

Testing Implications

Is that consistent with...?

What would be the consequences of...?

How would we know if that is true? How can we test that in practice?

Exploring Alternative Views

Is there another point of view?

Can you put it another way?

Are you and s/he contradicting each other?

What is the difference between your view and ...?

Scaffolding

What do you think about...? What is the reason for...?

If .... then what do you think about..? You said... but what about...?

Evaluating

Who can summarise the main points for us?

Can anyone say where our thinking has taken us?

What new ideas have developed?

If...why...?

Sustained Shared Thinking

Sustained shared thinking has been defined as

> " An episode in which two or more individuals 'work together' in an intellectual way to solve a problem, clarify a concept, evaluate activities, extend narrative etc. Both parties must contribute to the thinking and it must develop and extend."
>
> **Iram Siraj-Blatchford et al (2002) Researching Effective Pedagogy in the Early Years (REPEY) DfES.**

Sustaining and developing thinking – extending contributions

- Offering children information on the topic and encouraging them to add their ideas
- Inviting children to elaborate on their contributions
- Using reflective statements during discussions to encourage children to explore the topic further
- Short silences and increased waiting time before asking the next question
- Sharing your own experience and giving children time to respond
- Clarifying ideas to ensure everyone has understood what other children are saying, and to encourage others to add their viewpoints

From the study: "The Effective Provision of Pre-School Education (EPPE) Project: Final Report" by De Silva et al (2004)

 A project funded by the European Union and led in England by CDEC.

About the partners

Cumbria Development Education Centre (CDEC) is the leading provider of global education services in Cumbria, and is a member of the Consortium of Development Education Centres, one of a network of around 30 Development Education Centres across England. CDEC is concerned with good teaching and learning, emphasising a values-based approach and supporting thinking skills, enquiry and reflection. CDEC feels it is important for young people to understand the links between their own lives and those of people throughout the world, to recognise ways in which we are dependent on each other, to think about reasons for inequalities in the world and to find ways to act responsibly in their everyday lives. Alongside a number of national and global funded projects CDEC offers professional support and training to schools, outdoor providers and other education settings through outdoor learning, forest schools skills, philosophical enquiry, school linking, global citizenship and education for sustainable development. www.cdec.org.uk

Institute of Global Responsibility (IGO) is a non-governmental organization established in 2006 and based in Warsaw, Poland. IGO is concerned with both supporting initiatives and advocacy which address causes of injustice in the world and with providing quality development education. IGO believes that in education it is important to show alternative perspectives and solutions to global challenges and encourage critical thinking in young people and adults so that they feel they can make a difference. IGO seeks to present global issues in a way which enables pupils and young people to relate them to their personal experiences and thus develop empathy and solidarity with their peers in the world. IGO offers educational resources and workshops for teachers and awareness raising and advocacy campaigns for young people and adults. http://igo.org.pl/

Alliance for Regional and Civil Initiatives (ARCI) is a non-governmental organization established in 2006 with headquarters in Sofia, Bulgaria and five branches in other Bulgarian cities, including Silistra. ARCI initiates and supports actions which address development of quality educational programs for all age groups, cross-border cooperation and partnerships, which boost social and economic regional development. ARCI strongly believes in life-long learning as well as in open education that encourages free thinking and empathy. ARCI also works with the cross-border communities in Macedonia, Turkey, Serbia and Romania to establish intercultural partnerships and implement social and economic development projects. http:// argi-ngo .org/

The Future Worlds Center (FWC) is an incubator of social entrepreneurs who envision, design, and implement projects that promote the culture of co-existence, human rights, and peace, using methods grounded in the latest technologies, the science of dialogic design, and democratic dialogue. FWC's mission is to enable people to re-think and re-solve social challenges, both on the local and the European level. FWC's actions are positioned right at the edge of where social change can happen. FWC is an organisation in which ideas, projects, methodologies, and people are interconnected. Future Worlds Center has four operating units: the Global Education Unit, Humanitarian Affairs Unit, Futures Design Unit and the New Media Lab. http://www.futureworldscenter.org/

Introductory activities

1. Name game

Children explore their own names and their friends' names, and also the names of countries around the world. This is aimed at children aged 3–5 but will be suitable for those needing extra support with reading letters.

2. Questions for new friends

Children get an opportunity to ask questions of some of the new friends they have met through World from our Doorstep and their classmates, exploring the role of questions and the importance of good listening. This works well with 3–8 year olds – particularly the younger age range.

3. Cooperative drawing

Starting with looking at images of people cooperating, children move on to create a collaborative artwork. Suitable for all ages – can be a very simple creation or something more complex.

4. Welcoming Zogg to our school

Children welcome Zogg, visiting from planet Zargot, to their school. By introducing him and giving him a tour, they express their opinions on their immediate environment. Suitable for age 3–5 – developed with a reception class but could be a more detailed activity for older children.

5. I am special

This circle time activity introduces the children to alien Zogg, and looks at similarity and difference, supporting children to think about how we are all different. It is best suited to the early years phase, but adaptable to older children.

6. Stacking hands

This hand game, developed from WEDG's[1] "Growing Marigolds" publication, needs no resources and is a fun introduction for younger children to thinking about similarity and difference.

7. Exploring my neighbourhood with Zogg

This activity introduces the children to Zogg, visiting from the planet Zargot, and starts with reading his story "Meet Zogg". Children go on a real or imaginary journey to introduce Zogg to their neighbourhood, and then discuss their feelings about where they live while creating a visual display or map of the area. It is suitable for all ages – the journey, the discussion and the display can be adapted across the 3 – 8 age range.

8. Journey with Zogg or Thea

This activity takes the children on a journey with Zogg or Thea, learning about different countries and cultures. It is suitable for all ages – the journey, the discussion and the display can be adapted across the 3 – 8 age range.

---

[1] WEDG - Global Education Centre for East Kent

  A project funded by the European Union and led in England by CDEC.

1. Name game

Children explore their own names and their friends' names, and also the names of countries around the world. This is aimed at children aged 3–5 but will be suitable for those needing extra support with reading letters.

Subject/Curriculum links
Teachers have used this activity in geography, literacy and for getting to know each other.

Global Learning Aims include
Beginning to have a sense of their connections with the wider world, and between other people and places.

Personal Learning Goal
Children express their name and think about other countries. This helps them with self-awareness and social skills.

Starter activity

Provide a name tag for each child. Ask each child one by one their name, and write it on a tag while standing next to them reading out each letter. Each child then walks around the room holding their tag, introducing themselves and pointing out the letters.

Main learning activity

Ask the children to pile up all the name tags in the middle and sit in a circle. Pick one tag and pass it on to a child. The name tag travels from hand to hand being read, until it find its owner. Pass the next tag and continue until all the children have their name tag back.

Present the children with tags with names of countries from around the world. Make sure there are many countries to choose from, with at least one starting with the same letter as each child's name. You could include names of countries you learn about during this project (e.g. "Day in the life" stories from the project website: www.worldfromourdoorstep.com). Ask children to pick a country which starts with the same letter as their own name e.g. Angie – Angola, Ben – Belize, Zak – Zimbabwe, Tomak – Tunisia etc.

Spread the world map on the floor. Find the country on the map and encourage children to place their name tag there. Ask if anyone knows anything about that country – or has heard of it.

Based on Irena Majchrzak's PhD early years literacy methods.

To finish off…

Display the map and ask children to revisit some of the country names and remember where they are.

Resources you will need

- Blank name labels
- World map
- Blutac to stick labels on the map

2. Questions for new friends

Children get an opportunity to ask questions of some of the new friends they have met through World from our Doorstep, and their classmates, exploring the role of questions and the importance of good listening. This works well with 3–8 year olds – particularly the younger age range.

 Subject/Curriculum links
Teachers have used this activity as a whole class activity, getting to know each other, and with an element of physical activity.

 Global Learning Aims include
Being able to ask questions and listen to others.

 Personal Learning Goal
Children practise communication and listening skills, helping them with self-awareness, managing feelings, empathy and social skills.

Starter activity

Welcome all the children and tell them you are happy that you will have some time for playing and talking together. Explain that it's nice to tell others they are welcome and needed as part of the group, because everybody's contribution matters. Invite children to sit in a circle and take part in a warm-up game "It's great that you're here (with us)". The game is initiated by a volunteer who turns to a child sitting next to him/her and says: "It's great that you're here ...(followed by the child's name)" and they shake hands. The sequence then continues around the circle until it reaches the child that started. Then the direction is reversed so everybody can hear from each of their neighbours.

Main learning activity

You can start by reading through any of the three storybooks (Meet Zogg, Thea Discovers Chocolate, or Lily's Picnic). Then introduce a puppet, or toy, or one of the three main characters and tell the children that you have brought someone with you today to visit them. If questions arise organically let the children "talk" with the character. Ask the children: "Is there anything you would like to ask me about? Do you have any questions?" The less you speak as a facilitator the better – try to get as many questions as possible. Write down (or ideally get another adult to write) the children's questions alongside the names of the questioner.

After a period of questioning and conversation, analyse and cluster similar questions. Remind the children what questions were asked: "Agata asked if Zogg liked us", "Tomek asked what does Lily like to eat?" Then ask the children: "Why do we ask questions?"

Sum up different ideas and examples. We ask questions to, for example, find out information, to learn about people, to make contact, to chat. Questions can be about relations, feelings, opinions, knowledge, experience, facts, likes/dislikes, rules.

Invite the children to play a game. Tell them you will play some nice lively music. They can dance or walk around while the music is on, and when the music is turned off they should stop and ask a question to a child nearby and listen to what they answer. You can do several rounds of the game and then invite the children to sit in a circle. Ask children to tell you what they have found out from their friends that they spoke with. Ask if it was easy or difficult to remember what they spoke about, whether it was easier to remember their own questions or the answers and why? Ask for ideas of what helps to be a good listener.

Tell children their new friends can now answer their questions from earlier and any others they can think of. Ask them: "Can we ask Zogg/Thea/Lily about anything?" You can remind children of their earlier questions if needed. Play the role and answer the questions. If a philosophical question occurs Zogg/Thea/Lily can say: "This is really

  A project funded by the European Union and led in England by CDEC.

"The exercise It's great that you're here is a brilliant way to start any activity. Makes everybody in the group feel included and appreciated. Children like it a lot."

Daria Wodrowska, Przedszkole w Zielonej Górze, Poland

interesting, and I don't think there is only one answer to it. Different people can answer it differently. What do you think? And what do others think?"

To finish off...

Still playing the role of the character, say goodbye to each child individually. You can praise everyone for their questions and ability to listen to others.

If there is enough time you can ask children to draw a picture of one thing that they learnt/found out about their new friend or someone else today.

Resources you will need

- Puppets or toys of the three storybook characters
- Radio/CD player and lively songs
- Crayons and paper
- Pieces of paper and a pen or whiteboard for noting questions.

3. Co-operative drawing

Starting with looking at images of people cooperating, children move on to create a collaborative artwork. Suitable for all ages – can be a very simple creation or something more complex.

Subject/Curriculum links
Teachers have used this to support geography, art, life skills...

Global Learning Aims include
Being able to help and show care for others.

Personal Learning Goal
The children collaborate and experience feelings of pride and accomplishment as the finished product is a result of teamwork. This helps them with empathy and social skills.

Starter activity

In advance ask the children to bring in pictures from magazines or posters of people working together. Or provide a selection of images for them to choose from.

Display the images, and ask the children to select one to talk about. Begin by discussing the concept of collaboration and working together. Invite children to ask questions about the pictures and to look closely at what is going on in them. Try to identify the country it was taken in.

Place coloured stickers on the appropriate countries of origin on the world map.

Think about what the people are doing in each picture. Why are they carrying out the activity in the picture? Encourage the children to think about what happens next in the picture. Think of a link between the activity and your country if the image is from abroad. Can they think of a similar activity in this country?

Choose one image and cover the people in the image leaving just one person uncovered; ask the children to think about what it would be like for this person to do the work on her/his own.Following this activity explain to the children that they will be working to create something together.

Main learning activity

Option 1

Sit in a circle on the floor with the drawing/craft materials in the middle. Start by briefly revisiting one of the storybooks the children have enjoyed reading (Meet Zogg, Thea Discovers Chocolate, or Lily's Picnic), and choosing something the children would like to draw. This could be one of the main characters or anything else in the book – but everyone has to agree something to draw together – you could give the children the options and invite them to vote for one option. Count the votes and clarify what they will be drawing.

Explain that they will take turns to draw a small part of the chosen option. Continue until each child has had a turn. This can be done while listening to music, with the leader stopping the music at intervals to allow children to change over and starting the music again while the child is drawing/colouring. Repeat the cycle again as needed to complete the drawing and colouring if desired. Share the final picture and discuss both what the finished product looks like, and the challenges and benefits of working together.

> **"The children following this activity created together a list of rules for working together. They learned respect, patience and how to help one another."**
>
> **Eftychia Nikolaou Kolossiou 1, Public Nursery School, Cyprus**

  A project funded by the European Union and led in England by CDEC.

Option 2

Give each child a piece of paper, crayons and felt tip pens or craft materials. Choose something to draw/create or choose several options. For example, 1st, 4th, 7th child make a start on drawing Zogg; 2nd, 5th, 8th child start on a tree and so on.

Each child draws for an allocated time (marked by a rattle/bell, or music as in Option 1), and passes the paper or creation to the person on their left or right.

Continue until each child has had a turn on every paper. Share the final pictures/creations and discuss the outcomes/experiences of working together.

To finish off...

Revisit the images from the starter activity. Think about the differences between working alone and together. Some tasks may be better done alone or in small groups – some need large groups of people. What are some of the benefits of working together on a project (e.g. more ideas, different strengths and styles, fun)? What are some of the challenges (e.g. potential for conflict, feeling your bit might not be good enough, different styles)? And what skills do you need to be able to do it well (patience, listening, tolerance, encouragement etc.)?

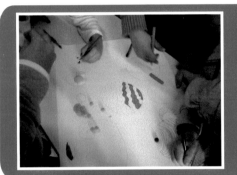

"We used this activity to introduce the concept of friendship and collaboration. We discussed how Zogg, the Boy and the Mouse all different kind of species broke through all obstacles and became friends and do things together as a team."

Prodroma Kleanthous, Geroskipou 2, Public Nursery School, Cyprus

Resources you will need

- Images, pictures and posters of people working together
- World map
- Drawing materials (crayons, felt tip pens, paints, colouring pencils etc.)
- Or craft materials for modelling
- 1 large piece of drawing paper or enough sheets for each child for option 2
- CD with music (optional) or rattle/bell or bicycle horn

Additional activities you may want to try

You may want to draw up a list of guidelines for working together as a class – a pledge for cooperation

4. Welcoming Zogg to our school

Children welcome Zogg, visiting from planet Zargot, to their school. By introducing him and giving him a tour, they express their opinions on their immediate environment. Suitable for age 3–5 – developed with a reception class but could be a more detailed activity for older children.

 Subject/Curriculum links
Teachers used this activity to introduce newly arrived children to the school, as well as projects describing the school.

 Global Learning Aims include
Ability to express understanding of a story or activity (Zogg's arrival), in relation to their own experience.

 Personal Learning Goal
Children become more aware of their own school surroundings and the roles within it. This helps them with self-awareness, empathy and social skills.

Starter activity

Begin by telling the children that a visitor is coming to your school. See if they can guess who it might be! Introduce them to Zogg with the puppet, or by reading "Meet Zogg".

Main learning activity

Discuss what the children think Zogg would be interested in seeing in the school. Make a plan of what the class want to show him in the classroom and around the school. Encourage them to think about times when they have arrived somewhere new – perhaps their first day at school or a new club. What helped them feel at home?

Make a book about places and things in your classroom or school that Zogg would need to know about during his visit, for example toilets, where to have dinner, where to play.

Then think about the people in your school who Zogg could meet – suggestions include lunchtime supervisors, the person who helps children cross the road, cleaners, teaching assistants, teachers, office staff. The children then take it in turns to go and introduce Zogg to various places and people working in the school, take photographs, and ask questions or make notes about that person's role.

To finish off...

Gather all the information children have found, and talk about it or make a display. Discuss how it felt taking a stranger round the school – did it make them feel proud? Do they think Zogg enjoyed it? Did they spot different things about the school when they were looking at it through Zogg's eyes? Are there any aspects of the school that children would like to change?

Resources you will need

• Zogg puppet/toy

• Meet Zogg book

• Digital Cameras

Additional activities you may want to try

You could develop this into writing an article for a school newsletter, or invite the school council or Governors to come and share what you found out, particularly any areas that children would like to change, or ideas they have for improvement.

 A project funded by the European Union and led in England by CDEC.

5. I am special

This circle time activity introduces the children to alien Zogg, and looks at similarity and difference, supporting children to think about how we are all different. It is best suited to the early years phase, but adaptable to older children.

Subject/Curriculum links
This activity has been used by teachers to support personal social and emotional aspects of learning, and for children in new classes to get to know each other.

Global Learning Aims include
Developing positive attitudes to difference and diversity.

Personal Learning Goal
Children develop a sense of themselves and others and build a sense of self-esteem. This helps them with self-awareness, managing feelings and social skills.

Starter activity

Introduce Zogg – you may need to read or revisit the book "Meet Zogg". Describe what he looks like, and emphasise how on the planet Zargot everyone looks the same.

Main learning activity

In a "circle time" setting, produce a mirror box. This can be very simple – a box with a mirror in the bottom – but if you want to increase the sense of special-ness and anticipation, you can decorate the box with beautiful sparkly shiny things. Explain that there is something very special in the box and that they are all going to get a chance to look inside. As the children pass the box around and look inside, they each see themselves. Use this as a stimulus for discussing similarities and differences between each other.

Give each child a blank book. On the front they draw a picture of themselves, and inside write three things they like about themselves.

To finish off...

Over the day or weeks, make time to revisit the books, and encourage each child to write something that is special about each child in their book.

Resources you will need

• Mirror box • Blank workbooks • Drawing materials • Zogg toy or puppet • "Meet Zogg" book

• Sparkly colourful materials and glue to decorate the box

Additional activities you may want to try

You could provide materials for the children to make their own mini mirror box – perhaps as a present to take home to share with their familes. This could be a simple small craft box with either silver foil or a mirror inside, decorated by the child with materials they like. This could encourage children to go home and discuss similar things with their family.

> "Children really enjoyed this, and it built up a sense of self esteem and appreciation of others."
> Teacher, Kingmoor St Oswalds, Ivegill, Cumbria, UK

A project funded by the European Union and led in England by CDEC.

6. Stacking hands game

This hand game, developed from WEDG's[1] "Growing Marigolds" publication needs no resources and is a fun introduction for younger children to thinking about similarity and difference.

 Subject/Curriculum links
Teachers have used this activity to build class cohesion.

 Global Learning Aims include
To express awareness of others, and similarities and difference, in relation to themselves.

 Personal Learning Goal
Children are encouraged to think about similarities and differences, and enjoyment of games of a more natural kind. It helps them with self-awareness and social skills.

Starter activity

Ask children what games they play – with each other, at home, on special occasions. List many games and talk about whether they all play the same games, or are some unique to one child?

Main learning activity

Divide the children into several small groups of about five. Sit in small circles. In each group one child puts a hand down followed by every other child in turn putting his/her hand on top, making a stack.

The first child puts his/her second hand on the stack, followed by the others until there is a tall stack including all the hands.

When the stack is complete, the child with their hand at the bottom slides it out and puts it on the top.

This is repeated faster and faster making sure the stack does not collapse. When it does, everyone generally collapses laughing!

All the groups can repeat this many times – practising the cooperation and communication needed to make it work.

You may want to give children the opportunity to draw or paint their own hands – either using handprints, or a detailed drawing picking out particular features, or paintings trying to match their exact skin tone. This forms a fantastic display to celebrate diversity and similarity within the class.

> **"Through this kind of game children come to understand the universal aspect of some games – no language is needed, no materials. It was a fun activity for the children."**
>
> **Ioanna Papantoniou, Elena Aristidou, Persa Petrou, Pantelitsa Zeniou Lemesos 8 Primary School, Cyprus**

---

[1] WEDG – Global Education Centre for East Kent

  A project funded by the European Union and led in England by CDEC.

To finish off...

Discuss with the children how they enjoyed the game. What did they like about it? What did they need to do to keep the game going? What made it collapse?

End the session with a discussion of their hands. Were everyone's hands the same? Are there any differences for example in size? Shapes of fingers and thumbs? Skin colour? Fingernails? Explain that all hands are in fact unique to us as individuals as we have fingerprints that no-one else shares.

Resources you will need

- Children!

- Optional drawing/painting materials

Additional activities you may want to try

You may want to read "Ebele's Favourite – a book of African games", and try some other games.

http://www.abebooks.co.uk/book-search/title/ebele%27s-favourite-a-book-of-african-games/author/onyefulu-ifeoma/

7. Exploring my neighbourhood with Zogg

This activity introduces the children to Zogg, visiting from the planet Zargot, and starts with reading his story "Meet Zogg". Children go on a real or imaginary journey to introduce Zogg to their neighbourhood, and then discuss their feelings about where they live while creating a visual display or map of the area. It is suitable for all ages – the journey, the discussion and the display can be adapted across the 3 – 8 age range.

 Subject/Curriculum links
This activity has been used by teachers to support learning in visual arts, outdoor education, mapping skills, language and many other areas.

 Global Learning Aims include
To understand that we are all part of the environment and our actions have an impact on it.

 Personal Learning Goal
Children become more aware of their surroundings and their place in the world. This helps them with self-awareness and social skills.

Starter activity

Start with reading the "Meet Zogg" story. Turn to pages 10–11 and focus on the two maps – Zogg's map of the neighbourhood, and Boy's map of his neighbourhood. Ask the children to identify particular features they remember from the story. If possible show a map of your country and also your local neighbourhood.

Main learning activity

Explain to the children that they are going to go on a journey around their neighbourhood or school grounds. Talk about how they might travel. Will they go by car? Will they walk? Cycle? Take a space ship? Stimulate a discussion about appropriate types of transportation – what's good and what's not so good about different methods. Which is most enjoyable? Best for the environment? Most exciting? Most sociable? How do the children prefer to travel and why?

Now ask them to think about taking Zogg around their neighbourhood (or school grounds). What would the children like to show him? What might he be interested in? Make a list of sights and areas to visit and show him.

The journey can be real or virtual. If virtual, use a map and photos if you have them, and talk them through going out of the door, and pretending they are taking the route past the sights. You could walk them around the room "looking" at the different things they pass and pausing to draw the view (either from memory or from the photos you have.

> **"This was a great opportunity for the children to see their neighbourhood in a different perspective from a visitor's point of view."**
>
> Antria Stavrou, To Proto Vima Nursery School, Cyprus

  A project funded by the European Union and led in England by CDEC.

If you are going on a real journey, children could take some photos of their surroundings, or stop to draw them – perhaps including a picture of Zogg in the familiar places.

Stimulate discussion during this journey by asking questions such as: What would Zogg think of this? Tell him what happens here. Describe what our neighbourhood is like – is it built up? Are there trees or buildings? Is it quiet or peaceful or noisy? Colourful or dull? Does our neighbourhood stay the same or change over time (i.e. through history, depending on whether it is a school day or a weekend, or by season)?

When you get back, encourage the children to look at each other's pictures. Collectively draw a large map of the area, including the places they showed to Zogg, with the pictures they took or drew.

To finish off…

Gather around the map to discuss:

- What do they like/dislike about their neighbourhood? Why? How can it be better?
- Does everyone think/feel the same about their neighbourhood?

Resources you will need

- "Meet Zogg" book
- Zogg toy or puppet
- Country map
- Photos of your neighbourhood
- Cameras or clipboard and colouring pens/pencils
- Glue and large paper or a large map of the neighbourhood

Additional activities you may want to try

Ask the children to imagine they are Zogg, and have just had a tour of the neighbourhood. Ask them to write a postcard or a letter back to Zargot telling their friends and families all about their visit. What would they say? What pictures would they send? Produce a display of the postcards around the map and photos/pictures from the neighbourhood.

"Children can enrich their knowledge and broaden their horizons. They learn to think beyond the narrow confines of their environment and express concerns on a global phenomenon."

Eftychia Nikolaou, Kolossiou 1 Nursery School, Cyprus

8. Journey with Zogg or Thea

This activity takes the children on a journey with Zogg or Thea, learning about different countries and cultures. It is suitable for all ages – the journey, the discussion and the display can be adapted across the 3 – 8 age range.

Subject/Curriculum links
This activity has been used by teachers to support learning in visual arts, social/life skills education, geography, maths, physical education, language and many other areas.

Global Learning Aims include
Beginning to have a sense of their connections with the wider world, and between other people and places.

Personal Learning Goal
Children become more confident about travelling and every day skills. This helps them with managing feelings, empathy and social skills.

Starter activity

There are two options with this activity – a journey 1) with Zogg or 2) with Thea.

1) Read the "Meet Zogg" storybook to the children. Explain that you are all going on a journey with Zogg to a different country just like Zogg, Boy and Mouse did when they hopped into Zogg's spaceship and landed in another country.

2) Read "Thea Discovers Chocolate" and explain to the children that they are going on a journey to a cocoa plantation just like Thea did.

Main learning activities

1) Ask the children to get into the spaceship and go on a journey. Ask them to imagine landing together in the same place such as the school field, local playground, park, riverside location or other places familiar to them children. Invite the children to describe the place that they have landed in. What is this place like? Are there any people? If there are buildings what are they like? Are there plants? Is it quiet/peaceful/noisy? Colourful/dull? What do you do there?

Encourage them to talk about what they like or dislike about the place, and why. How could it be better? Does everyone think/feel the same about this place?

After visiting a familiar place, the activity can be repeated landing in a different country exploring in detail. Perhaps even a different country each week! The children could be asked to research facts and images of the country in advance, or the teacher can provide resources. On the way you can learn about transport, about different climates, about different festivals – there are limitless possibilities! Children could choose the place to visit next – perhaps somewhere they have connections and could provide some information or photos. You could also combine this activity with learning about travelling and different types of transport – possibly including surveys of which transport class members use.

2) Using a large map and a bit of imagination, prepare the children to go on a journey with Thea – to Belize, to visit the cocoa plantation.

Discuss how they might travel, and where they might stay, and act it out (flying round the room with arms out as aeroplanes!). Mark each stage of the journey on the world map with string or coloured tape and pins or pictures.

Then discuss with them what that they will need to take with them on the journey. You could make the items...

  A project funded by the European Union and led in England by CDEC.

- Clothes, food etc. create little pictures or write the names of clothes, food
- Make suitcases/bags out of old boxes and string.
- Create tickets for aeroplane or boat.
- Passports with photos on
- Paper money/credit cards to buy tickets, food, clothes, petrol for truck etc. and act out the scenes such as filling the truck with petrol; staying the night at a hotel

Discuss the journey with them along the way. What do they see? They can draw postcards from different places on the way.

When you arrive – meet the cocoa farmers. What would you ask them? For example: How do you live? What is similar, what is different to your life? Do the children go to school? You can introduce them to a "Day in the Life of Alvaro Pop", a Fairtrade Cocoa farmer from Belize (http://worldfromourdoorstep.com/images/pdf/DayInLife/Cocoa_farmer.pdf)

Ask the children what they would take home as a souvenir.

Create a display with all the things they needed to take, drawings or creations of the favourite things they saw, around the map.

> "We linked this activity with the story 'The Little Prince' by who is also from another planet. Zogg and the Little Prince became friends and we all boarded Zogg's spaceship and visited each other's planets...Earth, Zargot and Asteroid 325."
>
> **Eftychia Nikolaou, Kolossiou 1 Pre-Primary School, Cyprus**

To finish off...

When the children "return" from their journey, support them to write and say thank you to someone they met on their travels. With younger children, record them saying thank you, or write their words into a speech bubble attached to a photo of them

Resources you will need

- "Meet Zogg" or "Thea Discovers Chocolate" books
- Used materials like boxes, newspapers
- World map, tape and pins
- Ideas!

Activities exploring interconnectedness

1. Community connections

Developed for ages 5–8, this activity involves families in exploring local connections in their community, and in creating a display and presentation on family connections.

2. Get creative with Zogg

This series of activities can be used across a number of lessons – each involves the children working together on a creative activity from modelling to making paper decorations, and reflecting on the collaborative approach. Suitable for 5 – 8 years.

3. Faces of the world

This photo activity involves looking at pictures of children around the world and discussing the movement of people and links between people and place.

4. Kim's game – what's missing?

This version of a traditional children's game introduces artefacts from around the world, and encourages children to look closely at them. Children from as young as 3 enjoy it, and for older children you can make it harder!

5. Where does food come from?

Looking at a range of packaging and photos of food, children discover that food comes from all over the world as well as locally, identifying the countries of origin on a map and expressing their opinions about different foods.

6. Breads from around the world

Through looking at breads from around the world, children get a chance to explore different traditions – and make or taste delicious breads! For all ages.

7. What's for breakfast today?

Starting with creating their own breakfast, and then looking at breakfast around the world, children think about differences and similarities, and also food injustice. Adaptable from 3 to 8 years.

8. Many hands make light work

This activity was developed in Bulgaria, using the preparation of a jar of Sunny Pickle as a stimulus for exploring where food comes from, and the joys and benefits of using local home-grown produce. You could use the Bulgarian recipe, or adapt it to a local seasonal delicacy – making elderflower cordial for example in the UK in May.

  A project funded by the European Union and led in England by CDEC.

1. Community connections

Developed for ages 5–8, this activity involves families in exploring local connections in their community in creating a display and presentation on family connections.

Subject/Curriculum links
This activity supports literacy and communication learning, specifically practising speaking and listening.

Global Learning Aims include
Children begin to have a sense of their connections with the wider world, and between other people and places. Concern for, empathy with, and sensitivity to others, locally and globally.

Personal Learning Goal
Children develop awareness of themselves and their communities, helping with self-awareness and social skills.

Starter activity

Invite parents to join in, perhaps as a "stay and play" morning. Children sit with their parents in a big circle. As a warm up activity, read out a series of questions, and ask children and parents to answer the questions by either standing and stretching up high (yes, a lot!), standing up (a little, or a few), or crouching and touching the floor (no, not at all).

- Do you eat chocolate?
- Do you ever visit a farm?
- Do you buy your food from a supermarket?
- Do you eat sausages (vegetarian or meat)?
- Do you build things out of local wood?
- Do you own something made from local wool?
- Do you grow your own food?
- Do you recycle?
- Do you consider where things come from?
- Do you smile?

Main learning activity

Start by reading "Lily's Picnic" together; you could invite volunteers to read each page. Invite discussion on what Lily discovered about the people in her community. Stimulate the discussion by asking questions like

- What do you think of Lily's new friends?
- Do you eat honey/bread/cheese etc?
- Where do you buy the food you eat? Who does the shopping in your house?
- Do you know where it comes from, how it gets to the shop?
- Can you get everything you need locally, or do you have to travel a long way? What can you get locally, what do you travel for?
- Do you think it's good that Lily's dad gave her some money so that she could pay for the picnic items she wanted? How do you think they would agree on a price?

Invite children to come to the centre of the circle and take an object out of a bag full of different items. Ask them to show and name the item to the rest of the group. Take the item to their parent. Together they find out where it comes from, look for evidence. Line them up according to the distance the object travelled to get here today. Encourage participants to look at what the other objects are and where they are placed.

As time allows probe with questions such as:

- Why do you think I have chosen these objects?

- What is important to you when choosing what food/produce you are going to buy?

- Where do you buy most of your food/produce?

- Are there some products we can't buy locally?

- What is fairtrade?

Sitting in a big circle again, explain that they are going to explore some of the connections – visible and invisible – between the people in their own small community right here. Invite one child or parent to share a fact about themselves, for example, where they live, what job they do, how they travel to work/school, where they play, if they are a brother, an auntie etc. They should start by saying "Hi my name is ..., I...". The first person to share a fact takes the end of a ball of string. Then invite other members to volunteer if they can think of a connection. Maybe people shop at the same market, or take the same bus route to work/school, or maybe a family member buys food from another family's shop. If participants don't have many obvious connections, be creative – we play in the same park, or like cycling for exercise. When a connection is made, roll the ball of string to that person, who takes hold of the string, and sends the ball on to the person who makes the next connection. Keep going until you have a criss-cross network of string connecting all the members of the circle. (If someone can't think of a connection, invite them to take the role of one of the characters in the story...they could be Alice who bakes bread to sell to one of the other children, for example).

Finish the activity by asking:

- Have you found out anything new about the people in our community?

- How does it make you feel to see the connections between us?

- What happens in a community if someone is ill, or sad? How can we support each other?

- Finally, reflect on some of the food and other items that children took out of the bag that came from outside our community, and ask participants if they can imagine how far around the world this network might be if we could see the visible and invisible connections between everyone.

To finish off...

Make a display of a map of your neighbourhood or town, marking important places that have arisen in your discussion with a pins and a labels. Connect them with the string, and add in other places too. Each child prepares a sentence about what they have learned about families of people in the class, encouraging them to get across the message we that we live in a "global village" and we need to understand, and appreciate and celebrate the people around us. Invite others from the school to come and visit, and show them the display and presentation.

Resources you will need

- "Lily's Picnic" book

- A bag full of commonly bought items (food, clothes, household, etc)

- Ball of string

- Pins and labels

  A project funded by the European Union and led in England by CDEC.

You could expand the activity by thinking about "differences and similarities" – showing photos of families from different places and traditions, for example: a selection of Scottish and Indian families. To avoid generalisations and stereotypes use phrases such as "some Scottish men wear kilts on special occasions" rather than "Scottish men wear kilts". Ensure that children are aware that items associated with a particular culture can be worn by others as well, and that fashion mixes items from around the world, and is constantly adapting and changing.

2. Get creative with Zogg

This series of activities can be used across a number of lessons – each involves the children working together on a creative activity from modelling to making paper decorations, and reflecting on the collaborative approach. Suitable for 5 – 8 years.

Subject/Curriculum links
Teachers have used this as an arts lesson, also for maths and numeracy, and for making decorations for their classroom at Christmas, or for a school party or fete.

Global Learning Aims include
Children will begin to understand how their actions affect others, and consider what might happen if they acted differently.

Personal Learning Goal
Children develop a sense of their role within a team, respecting and learning from others. This helps with motivation, empathy and social skills.

Starter activity

Start by reading "Meet Zogg" – or return to the part where Zogg meets his new friends on earth. Ask the children who their friends are. Stimulate a discussion about who can be considered a friend, how friends behave, how they work/play/study together. Are friends always similar? Zogg's aren't! Focus on tolerance and mutual respect as key to making and keeping friends. Following the discussion, ask some children to write words that describe friendship on the board. The class decide which are the most important for lasting friendship. Then ask the children to set up groups of four friends to work on a task.

Main learning activity

The first task is to make Zogg out of modelling clay. Each team member has to prepare a different part of the body by using the image of Zogg from the book. While modelling, the players also need to negotiate the dimensions of the body parts so when they glue together the clay, Zogg looks proportionate.

When the parts of Zogg are put together, the children are encouraged to discuss the steps they followed in order to reach a shared decision on the Zogg dimensions. They also share feelings and emotions during the learning activity, both positive and negative. The teacher briefly discusses the reasons for the "bad" emotions and they think about how they can overcome these on the next activity – perhaps through better communication, or checking how everyone is feeling as they go along.

The second activity starts by reading the football game part of "Meet Zogg". Ask questions about the game rules – this introduces the topic of "fair play". If you are working in a bilingual setting (as in Hristo Botev school in Bulgaria where this activity was developed) take care to ensure culturally correct explanations of "fair" and "equality" when working or playing together.

Then suggest a new task to the children: "Let's organise a factory which produces Christmas paper decorations". These are traditional Bulgarian decorative laces made out of glued strips of colourful paper – similar paper chains are also popular in England.

In this activity the teams are bigger – groups of twelve children have to organise an assembly line by negotiating production steps and production responsibilities.

A project funded by the European Union and led in England by CDEC.

The children, assisted by the teacher, organise themselves in a long production line to develop the class decoration:

How to make paper lace decoration

1. The first step is to prepare strips of paper. They should be about 2 cm in width and 12 cm in length. These sizes can be sketched on the paper with a pencil, or the paper could be folded in strips as a guide.

2. The next step is to cut these strips. It is recommended to have at least 50 paper strips, but there are no limits – apart from the size of the classroom!

3. A strip is folded into a circle and some glue is applied at the end to securely link both ends.

4. Another strip is inserted into the first circle to form a chain and after that glued.

5. Steps 4–5 are repeated until the needed length of linked paper strips is reached.

6. To make it more elaborate, start new chains by adding paper loops to circles at different points of the chain to form branches and connect them to form lace shapes.

To finish off...

The children get together, hang the decorative lace and congratulate themselves on finishing it. They start reviewing how they came to achieve such a beautiful result, how they feel about it and what they will remember from the team working activities!

Resources you will need

- "Meet Zogg" book
- Modelling clay for Zogg
- Sheets of colourful paper, packaging paper or recycled strips of paper
- Scissors and glue
- Pencil and a ruler

Additional activities you may want to try

To take the theme of co-operation further, the children who have completed this activity could devise a lesson to teach younger children or other classes to make their own chains.

"As the activity involves cutting geometric shapes, knowledge of colours, textures and patterns, it is also used for practising maths.

"Kids take pride in what they achieved as this activity allows them to organise themselves and take care of the whole 'production' of the decorations."

Adriana Dobreva, Primary School Hristo Botev', Alfatar, Bulgaria

3. Faces of the world

This photo activity involves looking at pictures of children around the world, and discussing the movement of people and links between people and place.

Subject/Curriculum links
Teachers have used this activity to learn about geography, cultural diversity, history.

Global Learning Aims include
To develop positive attitudes towards difference and diversity.

Personal Learning Goal
Children learn about movement of people around the world, helping them with self-awareness, managing feelings and social skills.

Starter activity

Mark world continents on the floor – don't worry too much about geographical accuracy! If you are outdoors use chalk, inside masking tape. Name the continents with the children and encourage them to visit each one to make sure they know where they are. Point them out on a map as well, so they can see what they look like.

Main learning activity

Distribute images of children from around the world. Give pupils some time to have a look at the photos before by asking them some questions:

- What do the children in the photos look like?
- Would you like to make friends with them? Why/why not?
- Are they all the same or different?
- What looks similar about them to us? What looks different?
- Is it okay to be different?
- What would it be like if everyone looked the same?

You could ask the children if there are any questions they would like to ask about the images or to ask the children in the images if they could.

Tell the children they can travel/fly around the world now. Put some music on. They can play aeroplanes with photos in their hands. When the music stops the children should "fly" to the nearest continent and sit down. Play the music again with children starting their journey with photos in their hands. Repeat the activity more times until the children, and those in the photos, have "visited" all the continents.

When you have finished, ask the children which continent they are currently sitting on. Begin a discussion about:

- Can you travel wherever you want? Can everyone? What stops us travelling? What encourage us to travel?
- Can we tell where someone lives just by their physical appearance? Is physical appearance connected in any way with the place you live in?
- How are people and places connected?

  A project funded by the European Union and led in England by CDEC.

Read a story that celebrates similarity and difference, such as "Hair Around the World Celebrating Diversity" in "Growing Up Global" RISC (Reading International Solidarity Centre, www.risc.org.uk/education).

Resources you will need

- Images of children with different ethnicities (you can find a useful starting point here http://www.kidsacrosstheworld.com/education/)

- World map

- Masking tape or chalk

- Music

4. Kim's game – what's missing?

This version of a traditional children's game introduces artefacts from around the world, and encourages children to look closely at them. Children from as young as 3 enjoy it, and for older children you can make it harder!

Subject/Curriculum links
Teachers have used this as an introduction to world geography, history and to develop observation and memory skills.

Global Learning Aims include
Respecting that people (including themselves) have different cultures.

Personal Learning Goal
Children develop awareness of the world around them, and use their own knowledge to make connections. This helps with self-awareness and empathy

Starter activity

Firstly collect artefacts with origins around the world. You could ask the children to bring in an artefact to show or bring pictures of artefacts that they are interested in. If you live somewhere near a Development Education Centre (in the UK) or equivalent, they will be able to lend you a box of artefacts. We have provided some pictures to get you started if you can't find artefacts.

Main learning activity

Place the artefacts on a table and invite the children to look at and touch them. (Perhaps display any fragile or precious things people have brought in from home separately, where they can't be handled and broken). Ask children if they want to tell the class about the things they brought in, and ask questions to stimulate discussion.

Then take each artefact and discuss it. Do they know where it is from? Does it have a particular use? Or meaning? Take out the world map and find the artefact's origin.

Now put a selection of items on a tray. Invite the children to look very carefully, as one item is about to disappear and they have to work out which one! Cover the tray with a cloth and instruct the children to close their eyes or turn away. Secretly remove one of the artefacts. When the children open their eyes, remove the cloth, and reveal the remaining artefacts. The children have to work out which one has been removed!

You can repeat this with children taking turns to be the one to remove an object. And with older children, not only do they have to identify which item is missing, but remember where it came from and what it is used for.

To finish off...

Discuss whether they found it easy or difficult. Did learning about the artefacts first make it easier? Finally talk about which items were familiar and which were not, and whether there are similar artefacts from their own country that they could use to play this game with children from another country? Which would they choose and how would they describe them?

Resources you will need

- Artefacts or pictures of artefacts (see those provided overleaf)

- World map

- Internet access or books to research the story behind each artefact

 A project funded by the European Union and led in England by CDEC.

Older children could pair up, take an item they are interested in, then research its history, culture, origin, and use then come back and present to the whole class.

> "They were surprised and excited to learn that many of the artefacts that they were familiar with are part of cultures from other countries."
>
> Maria Loizou – Pissouriou Primary School, Cyprus

Pictures of artefacts

Scotland

Cambodia

Hungary

Kyrgystan

China

Kenya

Chile

Irleand

 A project funded by the European Union and led in England by CDEC.

Jerusalem

Chile

Trinidad & Tobago

Egypt

Cuba

Germany

Haiti

South Africa

A project funded by the European Union and led in England by CDEC.

5. Where does food come from?

Looking at a range of packaging and photos of food, children discover that food comes from all over the world as well as locally, identifying the countries of origin on a map and expressing their opinions about different foods.

Subject/Curriculum links
Teachers have used this to support geography, art, life skills.

Global Learning Aims include
Understand that some of the food they eat comes from their own country , and some from elsewhere.

Personal Learning Goal
Children understand there are many different opinions on food. This helps them with empathy.

Starter activity

In advance, ask the children to bring in pictures of different types of food and bring in packaging from used food items.

Discuss the different foods with the children. Where does it come from? What's local and what comes from other countries? What would they like to eat or try? Do they all like the same things?

Main learning activity

Fill a reusable supermarket bag with food items, pictures or packaging from different countries. Display a large world map.

Invite the children to take turns to unpack the items, and talk about where the food item might have come from. Write the name of the item on a post it or sticky label and attach it to the country on the map where it comes from.

Display all the food items, photographs (including those provided) and packaging. Invite children to ask questions about these pictures and to look closely at what is going on in them.

Choose a photograph or picture and identify the food items and the country of origin. Can they find these food items here in this country also?

Place coloured sticky dots on the appropriate countries of origin on the world map. Discuss with the children how far away these food items have come to their country. You may also discuss with them examples of when some food items were not used to be available or produced in their local community and now they are (e.g. in Cyprus now avocados, guavas, bananas are now produced locally).

> **"We used this activity to introduce different cultural foods from different countries in the class. We also discussed the similarities and differences of the types of food. The children were really excited about this activity."**
>
> **Eftychia Nikolaou, Kolossiou 1, Nursery School, Cyprus**

  A project funded by the European Union and led in England by CDEC.

To finish off...

Stimulate a discussion using what they have learned about food. Emphasise that food is an important part of culture as well as a basic need, and that different foods are produced in different places. You could expand this to look at injustice around food – how sometimes food produced in one country is exported to other countries, and those growing it don't have access to it.

Resources you will need

- A reusable bag, preferably a "bag for life".
- A selection of items from different countries: tin, rice, dried fruit, sugar, coffee, chocolate etc.
- Post-its or sticky labels.
- Large world map
- Photographs of food items and dishes from around the world (being careful to avoid stereotypical images) including ones of people involved in food production activities from your own and other countries. Show the country of origin on the back of the pictures. A selection is provided on the worksheet opposite

Additional activities you may want to try

You may want to look at the stories of local food producers involved in the World from our Doorstep project (www.worldfromourdoorstep.com, choose "Classroom Resources"), or even invite a local producer to come and visit, or arrange a visit to a local farm.

This activity can lead to a food tasting session trying different foods from different countries, or from children's home traditions.

A project funded by the European Union and led in England by CDEC. 43

Food photo resource

 A project funded by the European Union and led in England by CDEC.

1. Nasi
2. Polish soup
3. Moroccan
4. Appam
5. Huevos

A project funded by the European Union and led in England by CDEC.

6. Breads from around the world

Through looking at breads from around the world, children get a chance to explore different traditions – and make or taste delicious breads! For all ages.

Subject/Curriculum links
Teachers have used this as a cooking activity, an art activity, and a history and geography lesson.

Global Learning Aims include
Children will be able to make connections between their lives and lives of others.

Personal Learning Goal
Looking at connections between their lives and those of others helps children with self-awareness and empathy.

Starter activity

Introduce the topic of bread by asking children what their favourite bread is, what kinds of bread they see in their local bakery or supermarket, and how many other kinds of bread they can name.

Main learning activity

Read some information about the history of bread, and how it is produced, at a suitable level for your class. We have provided some information to get you started. Talk about who makes bread in the children's families. Have they ever tried it?

Now either give out or show images of different types of bread from around the world (find some on the following pages), pointing out any breads the children mentioned in the introductory discussion. For each one, ask whether the children know this type of bread, its origin and if they have ever tried it.

Stick coloured dots on the world map to show where the breads come from, and talk about how so many countries all around the world have bread in their daily lives and how differently it is made in each part of the world.

Now provide the children with pieces of clay or play-dough and ask them to create different types of bread.

To finish off...

Try it for real! Pick a bread to make and bring in the ingredients and utensils to make and bake it. Making a batch of rolls or small loaves is one idea – children can each have a small amount of the dough, and make it in a particular shape to take home for their families.

> "I showcased more pictures of the way people bake bread. And then brought a lot of different types of bread for the children to taste."
>
> **Eftychia Nikolaou Kolossiou 1, Nursery School, Cyprus**

A project funded by the European Union and led in England by CDEC.

- Printouts (either hard copies or if the schools can accommodate use them on screen) of the different types of bread.

- History of bread information (included)

- World map

- Clay or play dough or actual dough

- Coloured dots

- Ingredients and utensils for bread making

Additional activities you may want to try

Look at the "A Day in the Life of a Flaounes Baker" (pronounced fla-oo-nez) on the World from our Doorstep website (http://worldfromourdoorstep.com/images/files/Day_in_the_life_Flaounes.pdf) and talk the children through the day of a local baker. Invite someone who makes bread to come and give a demonstration.

> **"The children realized that there are common elements in different countries from the activity 'Breads of the world'. They understood how something so common and obvious to us can mean something different to other people around the world."**
>
> **Irene Demosthenous, Chryseleousa Primary School, Cyprus**

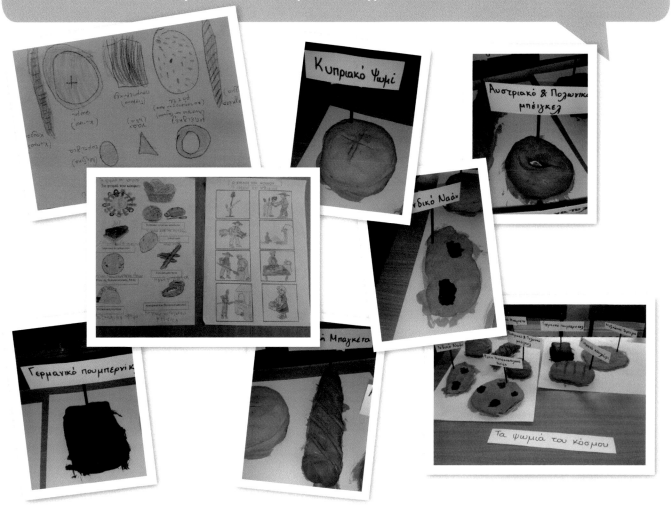

Breads of the world

Brief history of bread:

Bread is one of the oldest prepared foods. Evidence from 30,000 years ago in Europe revealed starch residue on rocks used for pounding plants. It is possible that during this time, starch extract from the roots of plants, such as cattails and ferns, was spread on a flat rock, placed over a fire and cooked into a primitive form of flatbread. Around 10,000 BC, with the dawn of the Neolithic age and the spread of agriculture, grains became the mainstay of making bread. Yeast cells are ubiquitous, including the surface of cereal grains, so any dough left to rest will become naturally leavened.

(http://en.wikipedia.org/wiki/Bread)

Kneading of bread in Boeotia, 5th century BC

The first kneading and therefore the first production of bread in its current form is likely to have been in Egypt about 3,000 years ago. Images of types of bread which are known to us today were discovered in ancient Egyptian tombs.

 A project funded by the European Union and led in England by CDEC.

Breads from around the world

Cyprus village bread

The difference between Cyprus village bread and other breads is the way the leaven is made, and the characteristic shape of the bread with the round notch around it. It is baked in the traditional oven and uses specific tools like the "fournoftio" a long wooden tool in which to place the breads in the oven.

Bagel

A bagel is a bread product originating from Poland, traditionally shaped by hand into the form of a ring from yeasted wheat dough, roughly hand-sized, which is first boiled for a short time in water and then baked. The result is a dense, chewy, doughy interior with a browned and sometimes crisp exterior. Bagels are often topped with seeds baked on the outer crust, with the traditional ones being poppy or sesame seeds.

Roti

Roti is an Indian subcontinent flat bread, made from stoneground wholemealflour, traditionally known as attaflour, that originated and is consumed in India, Pakistan, Nepal, Sri Lanka and Bangladesh. It is also consumed in parts of South Africa, the southern Caribbean, particularly in Trinidad and Tobago, Guyana, and Suriname, and Fiji. Its defining characteristic is that it is unleavened. Indian naan bread, by contrast, is a yeast-leavened bread.

Tortilla

Thin flatbread made from finely ground wheat flour. Originally derived from the corn tortilla (tortilla in Spanish means "small torta", or "small cake") A bread of maize which predates the arrival of Europeans to the Americas, the wheat flour tortilla was an innovation after wheat was brought to the New World from Spain while this region was the colony of New Spain. It is made with an unleavened, water based dough, pressed and cooked like corn tortillas. It is also used as a plate for holding in sauces, rice, vegetables, meats and more.

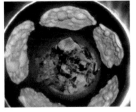

Naan

Naan, nan or khamiriis a leavened, oven-baked flatbread found in the cuisines of West, Central and South Asia. It is thought to have originated in India since the Tandoor oven (a traditional oven) in which it is made originated there. With the migration of the Roma people from India, it spread to other parts of West Asia.

Pumpernickel

Pumpernickel is a typically heavy, slightly sweet rye bread traditionally made with coarsely ground rye originating in Germany.

It is often made with a combination of rye flour and whole rye berries. At one time it was traditional peasant fare, but largely during the 20th century various forms became popular through delicatessens and supermarkets.

A project funded by the European Union and led in England by CDEC.

Mantou

Mantou, often referred to as Chinese steamed bun/bread, is a type of cloud-like steamed bread or bun originating in Northern China. The name, "mantou" is said to have originated from a tale about the medieval army general, ZhugeLiang. They are typically eaten as a staple in northern parts of China where wheat, rather than rice, is grown. They are made with milled wheat flour, water and leavening agents. Sometimes they are plain, sometimes they have filling.

Ciabatta

Ciabatta which means slipper bread due to the fact that its shape is like a slipper is an Italian white bread made from wheat flour, water, salt, olive oil and yeast, created in 1982 by a baker in Adria, Veneto, Italy, in response to popularity of French baguettes. Ciabatta is somewhat elongated, broad and flat and is baked in many variations.

Pita

Pita or pitta is a soft, slightly leavened flatbread baked from wheat flour. It is used in many Mediterranean, Balkan and Middle Eastern cuisines. Pita can be used to scoop sauces or dips such as hummus and taramosalata, or to wrap kebabs, gyros or falafel in the manner of sandwiches. It can also be cut and baked into crispy pita chips.

Baps

Baps traditionally made in Scotland are not sweet, unlike the Irish version, which may contain currants. The 9th Edition of the Concise Oxford Dictionary (1995) says that the word "bap" dates from the 16th century and that its origin is unknown. The most delicious way to enjoy them is straight out of the oven covered in lashings of butter.

Baguette

A baguette is "a long thin loaf of French bread" that is commonly made from basic leavened dough (the dough, though not the shape, is defined by French law). It is distinguishable by its length and crisp crust. It dates from the era of French King Louis XIV.

Draw your own favourite bread!

A project funded by the European Union and led in England by CDEC.

7. What's for breakfast today?

Starting with creating their own breakfast, and then looking at breakfast around the world, children think about differences and similarities, and also food injustice. Adaptable from 3 to 8 years.

Subject/Curriculum links
Teachers have used this as an art activity, a geography lesson, and in health education.

Global Learning Aims include
Children will understand that other people being healthy and happy can make the world a nicer place for all of us.

Personal Learning Goal
Expressing opinions about their breakfasts and those of others helps children with self-awareness, empathy and social skills.

Starter activity

Welcome all the children, sit together in a circle and ask them about their favourite breakfast. Invite everybody to share with the group and then to draw it on a piece of paper – or on a paper plate. Give them plenty of time to make it colourful, and include details such as drinks. When children are finished ask everybody to show their drawing and explain what their favourite breakfast consists of. You can encourage others to ask additional questions about the drawings. Remind them about the importance of listening to each other. When all have shared their breakfasts, stimulate discussion about diversity: does everybody like the same thing? Can any ingredient be used to make different breakfasts? Also introduce the idea of inequality and rights and needs by asking why it is important to eat breakfast. Is every child in your country able to have a good breakfast every day? And in the world? With older children support this discussion with some facts – such as "About 842 million people in the world do not eat enough to be healthy. That means that one in every eight people on earth goes to bed hungry each night." http://www.foodsecurity.ac.uk/issue/facts.html

Spread the breakfasts around the floor and ask children which are similar in terms of ingredients, and begin to cluster them. For example, all breakfasts including eggs in one area of the room, and all involving bread in another. There will of course be overlap and you may need to help them realise that scrambled eggs on toast could go in either category, for example!

Explain that they are now going to vote with their feet – you will read a statement and they will each walk to a group of drawings which are most appropriate to them.

Which breakfast…

- Is most healthy?
- They have never eaten?
- They would most like to try?
- Is the most delicious to them?

After each vote ask the children to explain their position. You may add information, especially regarding healthy food. You could ask the children in turn to think of a statement and try it out on their peers.

A project funded by the European Union and led in England by CDEC.

Divide the children into pairs or small groups and give each pair/group a photo of a child. Allow a few minutes for discussions about where the child might be from and why. Make sure that you use images and support discussion that challenges stereotypes about appearance and place – not all black people come from Africa, for example! Show each country on a map of the world, and name the continent it is in to help children with their discussions.

Spread the photos with breakfasts from around the world on the floor, and ask groups to try and find their child's breakfast. Then give them a few minutes to examine the breakfast, before asking them about the ingredients in the breakfasts. Where do they come from? How do we know that? It's worth going back to thinking about their own breakfasts which consisted of products not only from their own countries.

Ask the children to vote with their feet again. Find a breakfast which:

- Is the most healthy
- They would like to try
- It would be difficult for them to finish
- Can be prepared in their home

After each statement ask for reasons for their votes. Give others a chance to comment and ask additional questions – providing more information about the breakfasts. Give children the opportunity to change their vote in response to new information or opinion. Make sure that such a change is seen as perfectly normal part of a discussion and not as a defeat.

To finish off...

Gather back into a circle and ask:

- Why do children in different countries eat different things for breakfasts?

- Could we prepare all of these breakfasts in our country? Why/Why not?

- Is it good or bad that we are different, not only all over the world, but also in our country, and even in our group in school? What can we learn from that?

- Why do you think it is important that everyone in the world should have enough breakfast?

In the end ask everybody to have a quiet moment of reflection on what they learnt today. Ask volunteers for their thoughts.

> **"Children liked the activity very much. There were a lot of emotions involved in the discussions, some groups were not able to reach a consensus and others volunteered to help them, which was a nice change from the initial rivalry among the groups. Even in a big group that activity is easy to facilitate. I think it can, with certain modifications, be included in even youngest (3year olds) groups in preschools."**
>
> **Karolina Szczepańska, Preschool no.5, Wołomin, Poland.**

Resources you will need

- Photos of children from different countries and their breakfasts – this activity was developed in Poland inspired by an article in the New York Times "Rise and Shine" by Malia Wollan, and they used the associated photographs by Hannah Whitaker

- Map of the world (or a globe)

- Crayons and paper or paper plates

8. Many hands make light work!

This activity was developed in Bulgaria, using the preparation of a jar of Sunny Pickle salad as a stimulus for exploring where food comes from, and the joys and benefits of using local home-grown produce. You could use the Bulgarian recipe, or adapt it to a local seasonal delicacy – making elderflower cordial for example in the UK in May.

Subject/Curriculum links
This activity is particularly suited to cookery and healthy eating but brings in elements of geography and ecology.

Global Learning Aims include
Children develop cooperation skills, sharing and taking turns as well as collaboration over tasks.

Personal Learning Goal
Working together as a group, creating something for their families helps children with motivation and social skills.

Starter activity

In a circle, pass round a selection of seasonal fruits and vegetables, encouraging the children to feel them, smell them and look closely. Explain that the children are going to do an experiment and if it is successful it will be very useful and tasty for their families! Ask the children for help to prepare some food which they will eat together, which needs many hardworking hands!

Main learning activity

Discuss together which fruits and vegetables are typical for different seasons of the year in your country. Talk about which they are familiar with, which they prefer and how they like eating them. Give examples of different uses – in Bulgaria for example, bananas tend to be prepared as a delicious dessert, but bananas are used in some countries for savoury meals and soups. Think about why in your own country you don't grow bananas, pineapples, cocoa? Point on a map of the world where citrus crops grow, and bananas, and tea, and cocoa – remind them of the journey of Thea to Belize to discover cocoa, if you have read "Thea Discovers Chocolate". This could be expanded by showing pictures of tea plantations in India and rice fields in China, for example. Explain that vegetables can be used not only to prepare salads, but sweet creams, ice-cream, jam. Ask the children if their parents make their own preserved food, or buy ready prepared from the shop. And what kind of food they prefer – homemade or packaged? What are the benefits of buying ready-prepared food? What are the benefits of making food from local ingredients – from scratch? Develop a list of the pros and cons of each.

Depending on numbers of children and helpers, split into teams and the task is to prepare a jar of delicious sunny pickle – or other suitable product. The recipe and method for the Bulgarian salad is here:

Sunny Pickle

Ingredients:

1 cabbage, 1 kg carrots, 500g green tomatoes, 500g green pepper, 1 celery heart

For the pickle juice – for a 3 litre (large) pickling jar

4 tablespoons salt, 3 tablespoons sugar, 18 tablespoons vinegar, water

Preparation:

Wash the cabbage, tomatoes and peppers and cut into chunks. Cut the carrots into slices. Cut the celery into sticks. Mix the vegetables up and put into the jar. If you want to, you can add 2–3 cloves of garlic and a few peppercorns. Once you fill the jar to the brim, add the salt, sugar, vinegar, and pour in water to cover the contents of the jar.

Close tightly and leave the jar in a light (but not hot) place. The jar should be shaken several times a day (for 10 days) to allow the spices to mix well.

Then the pickles are ready for tasting. Bon appetit!

Use this opportunity for learning about safe food handling – perhaps invite the school cooks in to help? Before you start, talk about important rules for working with food. Why is it important to wash the products thoroughly? How should we be careful when working with sharp objects, or when we need to use the stove and oven?

Pause while arranging the vegetables, and talk about whether it is important just to be delicious and nutritious, or whether the look of the food is important. In Bulgaria while preparing their beautiful salads they agreed that "we should treat food as an artist – carefully and with love in order to draw a wonderful picture".

When the preparation is complete, talk about food waste. What are you going to do with the mound of vegetable peelings? Think of sustainable ways of using them – some waste products can be turned into other things. In cocoa production in Ghana for example, cocoa pod husks and fermented liquid are being used to make soap, animal feed, and even wine and jam! Can you compost the waste in school?

To finish off...

As the children prepare to take their beautiful products home, refresh their memories as to what they did and why, so they can tell their families, spreading the learning about how to appreciate resources and use them without wasting. Discuss what their product would be like if all the ingredients looked or tasted similar – each one has value and adds something unique to the finished product. You can finish by reading "Lily's Picnic" together.

Resources you will need

- Seasonal fruits and vegetables
- Images of packaged and homemade food
- Ingredients and utensils for Sunny Pickle
- Map of the world

> "During the lesson the children had the opportunity to experiment with preparation of winter supplies with various products– cabbage, carrots, tomatoes, celery, peppers, cauliflower. The emotion of the preparation of vegetables and their arrangement created an incredible atmosphere."
>
> Dilka Filipova – Kindergarten "Zdravets" Ihtiman, Bulgaria

A project funded by the European Union and led in England by CDEC.

Activities exploring fairness

1. Puzzle time

This activity starts with children completing a puzzle or task in unfair conditions, using the feeling this evokes to think about fair and unfair more widely. It is suitable for younger children (3 up to 8) but you can adapt it by making the task more or less complicated.

2. That's not fair

An introduction to the concept of fairness, this activity starts with children's own experiences, and begins to introduce the benefits of Fairtrade. Suitable for ages 5 – 8.

3. What's Fairtrade?

Starting with a story, the children recreate a journey across the world, and learn first-hand about unfair reward for labour. This activity is aimed at the 5 – 8 age group.

4. Who made your chocolate?

Using a collection of packaging from products containing chocolate, children find out the story behind the adverts – and meet the people who really made their chocolate! Suitable for 5 – 8 age group.

5. Fairtrade farmers

By role playing the lives of a family of cocoa farmers, this activity introduces children to the need to pay for everyday things, and the benefits of Fairtrade to farmers. It is more suited to the older age range 5 – 8.

6. Fairtrade market

Pretending to be banana growers gives children an insight into managing family finances, and also the benefits of Fairtrade to growers and producers. Suitable for older children of 5 – 8.

A project funded by the European Union and led in England by CDEC.

1. Puzzle time

This activity starts with children completing a puzzle or task in unfair conditions and using the feelings this evokes to think about fair and unfair more widely. It is suitable for younger children (3 up to 8) but you can adapt it by making the task more or less complicated.

 Subject/Curriculum links
This is a play based activity, and can encourage development of fine motor skills, as well as encouraging thinking about the wider world.

 Global Learning Aims include
Children come to know what is fair and unfair personally, and that we don't all have access to the same things.

 Personal Learning Goal
The experience and reflection involved in this activity helps children with managing feelings and empathy.

Starter activity

Explain to the children that they are going to be playing some games and doing some puzzles. But that it will be a bit different from usual and they need to think very carefully about how the game feels and try to spot what's different!

Main learning activity

The "unfairness" can be set up in different ways.

Option 1: Divide children into manageable groups (about 10 maximum – and you will need an adult with each group), and give each group a jigsaw puzzle. Use a world map puzzle to add a sense of the wider world. Sit each in a circle with the broken up puzzle in the middle.

Ask the children to take turns to throw the dice until someone throws a certain number, for example a 6. When a child throws a 6 he or she comes into the middle of the circle and starts putting pieces together – the adult helper counting and noting how many pieces they connect. While they are doing the puzzle, the rest of the children carry on throwing the dice until someone else throws a 6. At that point the children swap, the first one coming back to their place in the circle. Continue until the puzzle is complete.

Then announce the number of pieces that each child managed to put together. Some children will have put more pieces together because they had longer, or more turns – by pure chance. Ask the children whether this matters. How do they feel? Now announce that the children will be rewarded according to how many pieces they put together – one sweet/raisin/sticker per piece. Give them their prizes.

Now ask the children who got many prizes how they feel. Are they pleased? And how about those who got nothing? Does that feel fair? Why does it feel so bad? And what could the group do to make it fairer?

You may find that those who got many sweets or prizes share them with the others, or they may make suggestions about making sure everyone gets an equal turn.

 A project funded by the European Union and led in England by CDEC.

Option 2: The other way to do this activity is by groups competing together under unfair conditions. Split into small groups of about 5. Give each group a puzzle or a task to complete, announcing that there will be a prize for the first group to finish. Then give the groups different condition for their task. If using puzzles this could include giving puzzles with different numbers of pieces or level of complexity, or give the same puzzle to each but:

- One group has to do the puzzle with the picture facing downwards
- One group has to do the puzzle wearing gloves or mittens
- In one group children are are not allowed to speak to each other.

Option 3: Use a timer, starting the groups at different times – one several minutes after the other.

Stop as soon as one team finishes. There will be general cries of "It's not fair!" especially when they get their prize!

Ask the children why that group managed to finish their puzzle first. Is it fair that one group was given more time or an easier task? What did it feel like to be in the winning group? What did it feel like to lose? What would they change?

To finish off...

Gather the children together, and make sure those who have not had a reward get one now. Does that feel better? Encourage a discussion of fair and unfair, drawing out examples in the real world, and what could be done to make things fairer. You could finish by reading "Thea Discovers Chocolate" to link this to beginning to understand Fairtrade.

Resources you will need

- Enough puzzles for one per group (teachers can use puzzles that they already have or create new ones)
- World map puzzle
- Dice
- Timer
- Sweets, raisins or stickers

2. That's not fair!

An introduction to the concept of fairness, this activity starts with children's own experiences, and begins to introduce the benefits of Fairtrade. Suitable for ages 5 – 8.

Subject/Curriculum links
This can be used to develop language skills, think about geography, and personal and social education.

Global Learning Aims include
Children develop a sense of fair play and a willingness to speak out and take action if they think an action is wrong or unfair.

Personal Learning Goal
Thinking about what is fair and what is unfair, rather than just what is good for themselves, helps with self-awareness, empathy and social skills.

Starter activity

Read "Thea Discovers Chocolate" and discuss the concept of fairness from the story. Why is Fairtrade fair? Why is it better for the farmers, their families and their community? Ask the children to think of situations they have been in where they have felt things were unfair, or fair.

Explain that for this activity the children will listen to or read several statements, which will be placed around the room, and they will be given 3 small cards each – one with FAIR written on it, on the second UNFAIR and on the third NOT SURE. They will use these to decide and show what they feel is fair or unfair.

Main learning activity

Read out all the large statement cards (overleaf), or ask the children to read them out. Then give the children 3 small cards each (fair/unfair/not sure).

Place the statements around the room or inside the circle. Read them again, one at a time and ask the children to go and stand beside the statement, holding up one of their cards depending on whether they feel a certain statement is fair, unfair or they're not sure. Invite children to explain why they feel that the statement is fair or not fair. Then ask children who had stated 'not sure' if they wish to change their statement to fair or unfair.

Then read out the next statement and do the same thing, moving from statement to statement until you have visited and discussed them all, then gather back in a circle.

To finish off...

Stimulate a discussion about fair and unfair and how it affects us on a personal level. How does it make them feel? Is it always clear what is fair or unfair? What can they do if they feel something is unfair? Make a list of actions that children can take in class, at home and in the wider world to encourage fairness. For example, speaking out if someone hasn't got something they should have, or encouraging their family to buy Fairtrade products.

Resources you will need

- Large statement cards – these are provided

- Set of cards with FAIR, UNFAIR or NOT SURE written on them (one set for each child) – on 3 different coloured cards

  A project funded by the European Union and led in England by CDEC.

Additional activities you may want to try

The children could create their own statements to be judged fair, unfair or not sure. Or they could think about their own definitions for fair, and write these up and display them on a board.

> **"The children acquired lifetime values and attitudes and learned to seek justice in their daily lives."**
>
> **Ioanna Papantoniou, Lemesos 8 Primary School, Cyprus**

That's not fair activity sheet

I have to be in bed by 8 pm whilst my older sister can stay up until 9pm.

Some children have a lot of toys whilst others only a few.

I'm not allowed to eat chocolate right before dinner.

We always have to share our toys when our friends come over to our house.

A project funded by the European Union and led in England by CDEC.

My older brother is allowed to go to the park by himself but I'm not allowed to.

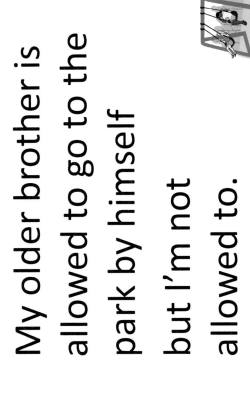

Many children have to leave their homes, friends, toys because there is a war in their country.

Some people work lots and lots of hours but get paid a small amount of money.

There are a lot of children in the world who want to go to school but can't.

A project funded by the European Union and led in England by CDEC.

3. What's Fairtrade?

Starting with a story, the children recreate a journey across the world, and learn first-hand about unfair reward for labour. This activity is aimed at the 5 – 8 age group.

 Subject/Curriculum links
Teachers use this activity to introduce world geography, understanding of how the world works, and also imaginative drawing.

 Global Learning Aims include
Children develop an understanding that other people being happy and healthy can make the world a nicer place for everyone.

 Personal Learning Goal
The group work and reflection involved in this activity help children with managing feelings, motivation, empathy and social skills.

Starter activity

Read "Thea Discovers Chocolate" with the children, and discuss each element of the story, finding out for example which bits children really like, what they need help to understand, who they would like to be in the story. Particularly focus on some words that might be unfamiliar.

Main learning activity

Then tell the children that they are going to role-play the book and follow Thea's route on the map. Ask the children to select which place on the journey they would like to talk about, and split them into teams based on this. Then two children are asked to role play Thea and her Grandma and the game can begin.

The groups of children spend some time thinking and possibly researching a bit more about the place they have chosen – the farm near Thea's Grandma's house, the cocoa farm in Belize, the Docks, the ship, the lorry etc. As Thea and her Grandma set off on the journey, identify each place on the map with pins and string, and give each group of children the opportunity to talk about their place, using questions to prompt, such as:

- Can you imagine yourself in this place?

- What would you hear, smell, see or taste?

- Is it warm or cold?

- Who might you meet?

- How do you feel?

Step by step trace the route of the chocolate and describe the sounds, smells and tastes of each stop.

Once Thea's route is pinned, thank each group for their presentations and "unevenly" reward or treat them by giving either one or three pieces of Fairtrade chocolate. Observe their reactions and encourage them to share their thoughts and feelings about their rewards.

- How do you feel about not having the right award for what you did?

- Do you find it fair or not? Why?

- Do you feel like giving another presentation?

- What would you like to do in a situation like that?

- What if you have to live on such an unfair reward?

  A project funded by the European Union and led in England by CDEC.

Explain that unfairness in payments leads to some people – often those who grow the product (for example the cocoa) going hungry and not having access to safe homes, good schools and decent health treatment. Then the teacher introduces the topic of 'Fairtrade' – revisiting the part in the book where the cocoa farmer explains the benefit of Fairtrade. Introduce the Fairtrade mark – found on products where the farmers are paid fairly.

To finish off...

The children then use their understanding of what's fair to imagine and draw a sustainable cocoa farm where all the producers are paid fairly and their families are happy. Make sure they all have the Fairtrade logo (image available in "Fairtrade Market" activity) somewhere on their picture!

Resources you will need

- A world map
- Colourful pins
- A teddy bear
- Drawing materials
- String
- Fairtrade chocolate

> **"Children enjoy being imaginary travellers and undertaking long journeys around the world."**
> **Mariana Gagova, Primary school 'Otets Paisii', Silistra, Bulgaria**

4. Who made your chocolate?

Using a collection of packaging from products containing chocolate, children find out the story behind the adverts – and meet the people who really made their chocolate! Suitable for 5–8 age group.

Subject/Curriculum links
Teachers use this activity to introduce world geography, understanding of how the world works, and also media literacy.

Global Learning Aims include
Children will be able to begin to identify unfairness and take appropriate action.

Personal Learning Goal
The group work and reflection involved in this activity help children with managing feelings, motivation, empathy and social skills.

Starter activity

The teacher asks the children in advance to collect and bring in packaging and wrappings from chocolate or products containing chocolate. Ask colleagues to collect packaging also so you have a good variety. The lesson starts by displaying all the packaging. The children are encouraged to go around, pick up a piece and read any information that says where and how the product was produced.

Main learning activity

Ask the children if they know who made their chocolate bars. Most children from the school in Bulgaria that tried this identified chocolate production with particular TV commercials– in this case a purple cow and a marmot from Switzerland, who promote the chocolate in the adverts! This can lead to an interesting discussion differentiating TV advertisements and reality – an introduction to critical literacy. Have a brief discussion about who the children think contribute to making chocolate – trying to name lots of different people.

Announce that today we are all going on a journey across the globe to find out who really made the chocolate. Gather the children round to read or remind them of "Thea Discovers Chocolate". Each time you meet a new person in the book, stop and ask the children what role that person plays. What do they do in the story of chocolate?

Ask the children if they know anyone in the local community who does a similar job – who works in a shop, or drives a lorry? Works on a farm? Works on a ship? When such people and jobs are identified, encourage the children to talk about what goods or services those people produce or transport and how they serve the community locally. You could also introduce some other characters using a selection of the "Day in the Life? stories (www.worldfromourdoorstep.com, choose 'Classroom Materials').

When you reach the Belize part of the story, focus attention on the picture showing activities in a neighbourhood in Belize. Read the description of the benefits of Fairtrade and its impact on community prosperity. As children talk about what they see in the picture, stimulate discussion by asking questions such as: What game are the children playing? Where are they? Who takes care of them? How do they look? Where are their parents? How do parents support their families? Do they go to school? Have a sports club? Visit a doctor if ill? Do they have enough to eat?

Revisit the description of the benefits of Fairtrade. Think about what might be different in the picture if the farmers there were not able to sell their cocoa to a Fairtrade buyer. There may be less money for healthcare, education, environmental projects – what impact would that have on the children in the picture?

To finish off...

Now it's time to return from Belize! Ask the children to help Thea remember her experience when she returns home, by drawing a detailed picture of someone or something from her journey.

  A project funded by the European Union and led in England by CDEC.

Resources you will need

- A slection of packaging from chocolate products
- Drawing materials
- "Thea Discovers Chocolate" book
- A selection of "Day in the Life" stories (www.worldfromourdoorstep.com)

> **"Children commented that Belize is a nice country, where kids play football just like in Brazil."**
>
> **Vanya Yankova, Primary school 'Kyril I Metodius', Silistra, Bulgaria**

A project funded by the European Union and led in England by CDEC.

5. Fairtrade farmers

By role playing the lives of a family of cocoa farmers, this activity introduces children to the need to pay for everyday things, and the benefits of Fairtrade to farmers. It is more suited to the older age range 5 – 8.

Subject/Curriculum links
This is a great activity for promoting financial literacy and maths.

Global Learning Aims include
Children develop cooperative skills, sharing and taking turns as well as collaboration over tasks.

Personal Learning Goal
Acting out a week in the life of cocoa farmers helps the children with motivation, empathy and social skills.

Starter activity

Read or revisit "Thea Discovers Chocolate". Examine closely the images that show life in Belize. Talk about life for the family of the cocoa farmer and the difference Fairtrade makes. The farmer explains to Thea that Fairtrade means he always gets a fair price for his cocoa beans, so he has enough money to feed his family and make sure everyone is healthy. And also all the children in the village can go to school. Fairtrade farmers can get clean water to their villages and build a doctor's surgery.

Ask the children to get into pairs, and using the pictures from the book identify similarities and differences between their lives and village life in Thea's story. Gather ideas from the children and write them up under two columns – similarities, and differences.

Main learning activity

Separate the children into two groups. One group will be a family of Fairtrade cocoa farmers and the other group will be a family of non-Fairtrade cocoa farmers. Give each group five beanbags or something to represent sacks of cocoa beans.

Give out the category headings – one set to each family, explaining that their household expenses will fall into these categories. Place the two sets of cost of living cards on a central table and give each family some time to sort them into categories and think about what each means. Please note that the cost of 2 coins for everything is used because it is easy for even young children – if you are working with older children vary the costs of items to make them more realistic.

Explain that:

- One child or teacher will be the cocoa bean buyer and they will pay the Fairtrade farmers 20 coins for a bag of cocoa beans and in turn pay the non-Fairtrade farmers 12 coins

- The families can sell their beans at any time

- Each family will have to pay their expenses with the money that they receive from the cocoa bean buyer.

Start by each family selling a bag of beans to get them started.

Now begin to describe a week in the life of a farming family. You may want to make this up in advance or improvise! Start with breakfast – each family needs to buy some food for the week (pause while a member of each family comes forward and exchanges some "money" for a food card). Make up a story involving washing day children starting school and needing equipment; a family member falling ill; the village water becoming contaminated and needing to buy water etc. As families run out of money they sell more cocoa beans. Stop every

  A project funded by the European Union and led in England by CDEC.

now and then and ask how much money and how many sacks of beans they each have left. Eventually the non-Fairtrade famers will not have enough money to pay for the things they need. Stop the game at that point.

To finish off...

Talk with the children about how they enjoyed the game – did they find it fun? Stressful? Why can the Fairtrade farmer afford to pay all of their expenses and still have cocoa left to sell, whilst the non-Fairtrade farmer can't even afford to pay for their expenses? Reflect that we can help more farmers get involved in Fairtrade by choosing Fairtrade products where possible – the more demand there is, the more farmers can sell their cocoa into the Fairtrade system.

Resources you will need

- Several copies of "Thea Discovers Chocolate", or photocopied images from the book
- Cost of living cards, laminated – two sets
- Cost of living categories cards
- Fake money/monopoly money, or tokens or beans to use as money/coins
- Bean bags
- Food cards

Additional activities you may want to try

This activity could also be combined with a wider discussion about the cost of living. Do they know how much households in their own country pay for living expenses? And how much do they really cost in Belize? Research the costs of basic items such as a loaf of bread, milk, a football, medicines etc.

Doctor 2 coins

Medicine 2 coins

Check-ups 2 coins

Books 2 coins

Pencils 2 coins

Erasers 2 coins

School clothes 2 coins

Food 2 coins

Washing soap 2 coins

Clothes 2 coins

Electricity 2 coins

Water 2 coins

Maintenance 2 coins

A project funded by the European Union and led in England by CDEC.

Health

School

Family Expenses

House Expenses

A project funded by the European Union and led in England by CDEC.

6. Fairtrade market

Pretending to be banana growers gives children an insight into managing family finances, and also the benefits of Fairtrade to growers and producers. Suitable for older children of 5 – 8.

Subject/Curriculum links
This activity has been used to introduce the idea of buying and selling, promoting financial literacy and maths as well as learning about Fairtrade.

Global Learning Aims include
Children develop a sense of fair play and a willingness to speak out and take action.

Personal Learning Goal
Pretending to be banana farmers helps the children with motivation, empathy and social skills.

Starter activity

This is a "let's pretend" activity – explain to the children that they live in the Windward Isles and are banana farmers. Find where the Windward Isles are on a map or globe, and show some images to discuss what life might be like there.

Main learning activity

Split children up into "family groups" of 4 or 5. They sit around the table in their own "home". Go through the Power Point presentation to show the market and the shop. Explain that you – the teacher – will play the market trader, standing under the Power Point slide.

Each family is given a laminated picture of bananas that they have grown.

One child takes the banana to the market trader and is given 10 coins. They go home and count their money with their family.

Meanwhile change the market into the shop, laying out the products they can buy. Add price tags to the items – their values are shown on the worksheets.

Now it is time to spend their money. The shop items are everyday items which they need to stay healthy and well fed and properly clothed: meat, milk, bread, vegetables, fruit, and clothing. The slide shows the different items, and the family discuss which they need and makes a shopping list. They don't see the costs of the items until they come to the shop. In turn each family comes up and tries to buy the items on their list – they can only spend their 10 coins. If they can't afford their initial shopping list, they need to go back to their family, having noted down the costs, and decide what to cross off.

Shoppers take their list back to the shop and buy the items (give them the laminated shop items).

When each family has done this, have a discussion all together – do they have everything they need? What's missing? Can they be happy and healthy with what they've bought?

Return all the items and start again. This time, give each family a bunch of bananas with Fairtrade stickers on! The market reappears. When the family come to sell their Fairtrade bananas they get 15 coins instead of 10.

Repeat the shopping process – they should find that they have the money to buy more items this time.

Once the shopping is complete, regroup for a discussion. Do they have everything they need now? What was the difference? How did the Fairtrade sticker make a difference? What did this mean? They were given a good price for their bananas so they could afford to meet their needs and be healthy and happy. Fairtrade can make the difference between a healthy well-balanced diet and an inadequate one.

  A project funded by the European Union and led in England by CDEC.

To finish off...

In addition, with Fairtrade, growers are given some bonus money to help their local community. Give each group another 2 coins and show them the slide or pictures showing some of the things they could spend it on – a health clinic, schools, a well, a nature reserve for example. What would they choose? As a family they can't afford anything, but by clubbing together and pooling their resource as a community, they can. Decide what would be the top priority for the community.

Resources you will need

- Picture of laminated bananas x 6
- Picture of laminated bananas with Fairtrade stickers x 6
- Laminated versions of shop items x 6 of each, for example milk, bread, vegetables, fruit, clothing, meat (overleaf)
- Shopping list sheets
- Coins or tokens or pretend money
- Powerpoint saying 'Market' with picture of banana market
- Powerpoint saying shop with images of what they can buy and prices
- Powerpoint slide of extra things they might get with premium: health clinic, schools, water well, nature reserve
- World map
- Images of Westward Isles
- Price tags

Additional activities you may want to try

Introduce new products e.g. TV, mobile phone, toys, and lead into a discussion of needs and wants. Or now you have decided what to spend your Fairtrade bonus on – the clinic, the school, the well or the nature reserve, do some research and design, draw or build a model of it.

Our shopping list

Item	Cost
Total	

A project funded by the European Union and led in England by CDEC.

Meat: 4 coins

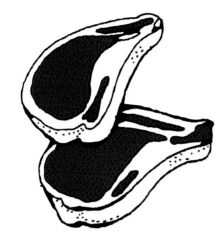

Milk: 2 coins

Clothes: 4 coins

Fruit: 3 coins

Bread: 1 coins

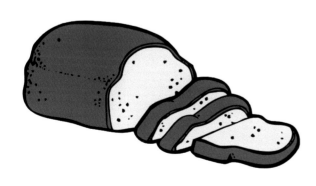

Vegatables: 1 coins

A project funded by the European Union and led in England by CDEC.

FAIRTRADE

 A project funded by the European Union and led in England by CDEC.

Shop

Vegatables: 1

Milk: 2

Bread: 1

Clothes: 4

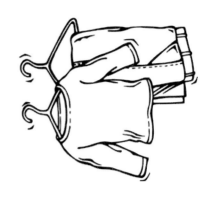

Fruit: 3

Meat: 4

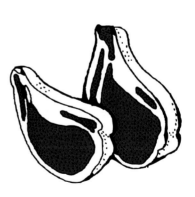

A project funded by the European Union and led in England by CDEC.

Market

 A project funded by the European Union and led in England by CDEC.

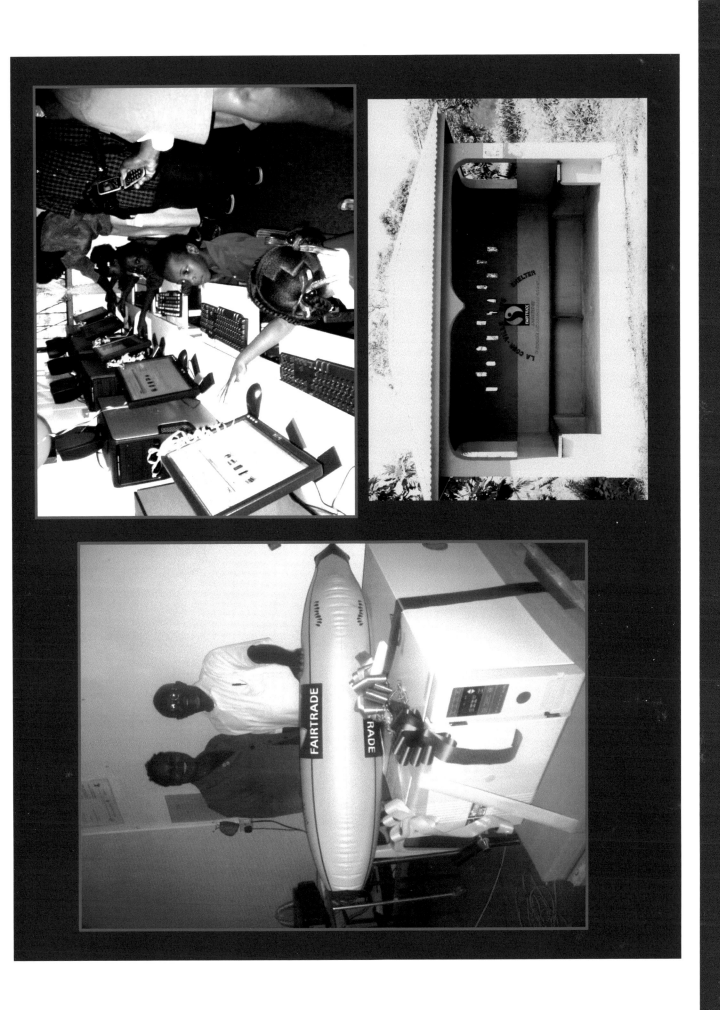

A project funded by the European Union and led in England by CDEC.

Activities exploring sustainability

1. Appreciating the world

This is an outdoor activity which aims to encourage an appreciation of the world around us, and foster a sense of responsibility for the environment and for sustainable use of resources through experiential learning. It can take place in the school grounds or in a local park and children from as young as 3 can take part with help.

2. Colours of the rainbow

This activity looks at colours that occur in our natural environments and human made environments around the world, and gives children as young as 3 the opportunity to find and paint everyday objects.

3. Fruitcake frenzy

This activity uses the metaphor of a fruitcake to explore what happens when we try and get treats for ourselves without thinking of others or the environment.

4. Mapsticks

This activity is about the children creating their own story sticks by collecting natural items on a walk either around the school or in a local park. Children from as young as 3 can take part with help.

5. Gifts from the sea

Using the sea as a stimulus, this activity gives you free reign to follow the interests and abilities of you and your students in an exploration of the importance of the marine environment, and how we can look after it. Pick simpler elements of the activity for younger children in the 5 – 8 age range.

6. Zogg's spaceship

This is an active game which can be played indoors or outdoors, for a minimum of 12 children. Children travel round the universe in improvised spaceships before having to negotiate what objects they can take with them on their journey – leading to an introduction of the concept of sustainability and the difference between needs and wants.

7. Zogg's house

This junk modelling activity starts by uses Zogg's example of re-using junk to make a house, and explores what makes a house a home. The age range 3–8 could all get something out of this activity.

8. Sustainable table

Making the link between locally produced food and delicious traditions, children and their families collaborate to share their favourite traditional dishes – learning about sustainable food choices along the way. With support from their families, even the youngest can join in.

9. Planet earth – learning from Zargot!

Using the excellent examples from Zargot, of re-using old materials, this activity involves cooperation to make footballs from old plastic bags – among other things! Suitable for 5 – 8 year olds – or younger children with more help.

 A project funded by the European Union and led in England by CDEC.

1. Appreciating the world

This is an outdoor activity which aims to encourage an appreciation of the world around us, and foster a sense of responsibility for the environment and for sustainable use of resources through experiential learning. It can take place in the school grounds or in a local park and children from as young as 3 can take part with help.

 Subject/Curriculum links
An outdoor activity – would tie in well in England with the Forest Schools programme or environmental education in general.

 Global Learning Aims include
Children recognise the difference between things that are natural, and things that are made by people, and develop a sense of their place in their environment.

 Personal Learning Goal
Seeing their local environment from a different perspective helps develop self-awareness and social skills.

Starter activity

Find a peaceful place outside and sit in a circle on the ground. Explain that this session is about exploring the "World from our Doorstep". Ask the children to look around and pick a word that explains how they are feeling right now. Share the words, acknowledging negative as well as positive emotions. Ask the children to try to locate where that feeling is, for example, if they say "happy", ask them where in their body is that happiness – their head, their heart, their tummy, their hands etc?

Main learning activity

Remind the children of how they make sense of the world – we have five senses, and today we are going to focus on some of them.

Activity 1 – Magic listening stones

- Ask children to stop and listen.

- Invite them to close their eyes and listen really carefully – what sounds can they hear? If they are finding it difficult to concentrate, tell them you have some magic listening stones, and invite every child to take a stone.

- Invite the children to hold the listening stones to their ears to help focus their sense of hearing

- What can they hear?

- How many natural sounds can they hear?

- How many unnatural sounds can they hear?

- How do the sounds make them feel? Write these down on laminated leave shapes and attach to a 'feeling' tree with string

- What would it be like without sounds?

- Ask questions and talk about the different sounds

Activity 2: Feely bags

- Give each pair/group of children a feely bag (a cloth bag they can put their hand in).

- Ask children to observe the different natural things in the environment.

- Ask each group to select one item, go and get it, and place it in their feely bag.

- Sit in a circle and pass each feely bag around in turn.

- Invite the children to guess what is inside by touch alone.

- What does it feel like? Is it hard or soft? Is it smooth or rough? Is it regular or irregular? Does it feel damp? Is it crackly or crunchy?

- Encourage children to think about how each item they have found is important to nature/people. Use sustained shared thinking and questioning to develop a dialogue.

Activity 3: Frames

- Children work in pairs.

- Give each pair a laminated or card picture frame

- Explain that they are to go on an exploration of the area (remind them of how to stay safe!), and use the picture frames to pick out different aspects of the view. It can be big/small, beautiful/ugly, natural/human-made, interesting/boring etc. Ask them to think about what they can see through the frame, what do they notice, what do you wonder, what questions would you like to ask, do you like it?

- When they return, ask each pair to decide which view they liked best, and tell the rest of the group, giving reasons.

- Encourage the children to think about the fact that they were all doing the same activity in the same environment, but they all found different ways of seeing the world.

To finish off…

End by asking the children, again, to think of a word that describes the environment that they have just been exploring using their senses, and ask them how they feel about that environment. Reminding the children that this is just one kind of environment on the planet. You could ask them to think of other types of environment (e.g. mountains, deserts, under the sea, forests, towns, cities, farmland, beach etc.) and how the environment can take care of us, make us happy, protect us, feed us, keep us warm/cool, and that we need to take care of it carefully as well.

Resources you will need

- A collection of "magic listening stones" (one for each child)

- A collection of laminated leaf shapes, on strings to tie to a tree

- Drywipe pens

- A collection of feely bags (not transparent, big enough for an object and a small hand to fit inside!)

- Laminated frames, all the same or in a selection of different shapes

---

 A project funded by the European Union and led in England by CDEC.

2. Colours of the rainbow

This activity looks at colours that occur in our natural environments and human made environments around the world, and gives children as young as 3 the opportunity to find and paint everyday objects.

 Subject/Curriculum links
An art activity which involves learning about geography and the environment.

 Global Learning Aims include
Being able to recognise the difference between things that are natural and things that are made by people.

 Personal Learning Goal
Thinking about ourselves as both observer and an integral part of the environment helps with self-awareness, empathy and social skills.

Starter activity

Start by reading "Meet Zogg", or revisiting it. Each time you get to a different place in the story, pass the book round and ask the children what coloured things they see – a red suitcase; a brown tree trunk, green Zogg, Boy's yellow hair. Write a description of the "thing" and colour of each on a card and ask the children it is natural, or made? Or not sure?

Main learning activity

Return to the page of Boy's neighbourhood, and the page showing the place far away where Zogg, Boy and Mouse land next. Discuss the different colours in the environment and the people around them that they see in the different places. How different or similar are the colours from our environment around our school? Let's go and find out!

Give each child a palette and three colours on a paint colour chart – each can be different. Take the children outside either around the school or further afield. Ask them to find something in the environment that matches each of their three colours. Ask them to paint these things on separate pieces of paper.

When you are back in the classroom, talk about the different colours. Which occur naturally in the environment? Which colours are common for non-natural things? Discuss that some things start as natural materials but have been made into other things. Metal for making post-boxes, for example, is mined from the earth originally. Even plastic uses naturally occurring oil. Rubber for car tyres originally from trees. Natural means in its natural state, but in fact most things we rely on have their origins in the natural world.

Encourage children to think about what is available in different environments and what it would be like if we could only use the things that exist on our doorstep to make everything else we need. Some people use much less of the world's resources than others.

To finish off...

You could close this activity by looking at the picture on page 21 of "Meet Zogg" and talk about the colours that Mouse and Boy could see as they walked home.

Resources you will need

- Laminated palettes – this can simply be laminated card
- Sample wall paint colour cards
- Meet Zogg book
- Painting materials: brushes, paint, card or paper

3. Fruitcake frenzy

This activity uses the metaphor of a fruitcake to explore what happens when we try and get treats for ourselves without thinking of others or the environment.

 Subject/Curriculum links
This activity can be used as a creative (and then destructive!) project (i.e. making a cake) and introduces concepts such as sustainable development.

 Global Learning Aims include
Children come to know what is fair and unfair personally, and that we don't all have access to the same things.

 Personal Learning Goal
The experience and reflection involved in this activity help children with self-awareness, managing feelings, empathy and social skills.

Starter activity

This activity was developed using a real fruitcake – which then gets destroyed as children extract delicacies from it, with the children then reflecting on the destruction they have caused! However, if the concept of destroying a beautiful fruitcake is too uncomfortable, you could make the 'fruitcake' out of play-dough, with non-edible treasured hidden inside. This would make a very good introduction to the activity – starting by making the 'cake' together. Deciding what goes in it, decorating it, and admiring it.

Main learning activity

Ask the children to sit in a circle. Put a tray with the fruitcake in the middle of it – a delicious and beautiful cake with lots of delicacies – fruit and nuts hidden within it. Ask the children to describe it, admire it – does it look like something they are proud of making, or would like to eat (if a real cake)? Then tell the children their task is to try and get the most pieces of fruit and nuts from the cake within a certain time.

Children start on a given signal, trying with any means possible to get the most treasures from the cake, putting them in their own small pots or cups.

When the time is up, ask them to count their treasures or delicacies. Who got the most? But instead of congratulating them, ask the children to look back at the cake. What has happened to it? It is likely now to be a pile of crumbs or a mush of play-dough – nothing like the beautiful item at the start. Invite the children to share their observations of how everyone behaved and what has happened:

- What does the fruitcake look like now?

- Children were proud of it before, or wanted to eat it. Do they still?

- Seeing the fruitcake now, how do they feel?

- What is more important: the cake, the delicacies or are both equally important to enjoying the fruit cake?

- Is it possible to share and enjoy the cake without destroying it?

- What could be done differently?

82 **A project funded by the European Union and led in England by CDEC.**

To finish off...

The discussion at the end should focus on ways that the good things in life can be shared fairly among people without needing to fight over them, thus destroying the thing for everyone.

Resources you will need

- Fruitcake

- Plastic tablecloth

- Food tray

- Small pots for delicacies. (If making a pretend cake, you will need play dough or equivalent, and treasures to hide inside.)

Additional activities you may want to try

Find some images or video clips about mining and quarrying, and explore similarities and differences between the game and what happens in those processes. Who are the winners and losers?

4. Mapsticks

This activity is about the children creating their own story sticks by collecting natural items on a walk either around the school or in a local park. Children from as young as 3 can take part with help.

 Subject/Curriculum links
An outdoor activity – would tie in well in England with the Forest Schools programme or environmental education in general.

 Global Learning Aims include
Children recognise the difference between things that are natural, and things that are made by people, and develop a sense of their place in their environment.

 Personal Learning Goal
Seeing their local environment from a different perspective helps develop self-awareness and social skills.

Starter activity

Explain that Mapsticks were used by Native Australians to communicate ideas to each other. Find and show some pictures, and also a mapstick you have made earlier. The stick acts as both a map and a story telling device. Explain that the children are going to go on an adventure and create their own mapsticks.

Main learning activity

Go outside into the school grounds or a local park or forest. Group the children into small groups of 3 – 5 each with a leader. Give each child or group a stick about 45 cm long – or if you are out in the woods they can find their own.

Follow a path or trail. As you walk, encourage children to look for items from nature such as feathers, twigs, dried leaves, pine cones etc. along the way. When they find something, the group leaders can help children attach the different items collected on to their stick. You can make one stick per child, or one per group. Some items you should not pick such as living plants, and make sure teachers are watching out for things children shouldn't touch such as toadstools.

When back in school encourage the children to discuss their findings and share/describe the item with the others. Ask them: Why did they pick up that specific item? Where did they find it? Why is it special? What story does it tell?

Invite children to look closely at each other's mapsticks and ask questions. Use sustained shared thinking to develop a dialogue, comparing the sticks and remembering the places where things were found.

To finish off...

The children may use all the items they have gathered and create a display to tell the story of their adventure.

Resources you will need

- A stick about 45cm in length for each group leader or each child
- String and or coloured wool
- A mapstick you have made earlier

  A project funded by the European Union and led in England by CDEC.

Additional activities you may want to try

Unnatural items such as litter could be collected (by the leaders wearing gloves) and brought back to compare natural and unnatural items and for talking about "Looking after the place we live in". You could combine it with a litter picking project, encouraging children to take care of their own environment. If you are walking in a public place, and there is litter, the children could design a poster asking people to pick up their litter, which can be laminated and attached to a fence post or tree – remember to go and remove it in a few weeks or it will become litter itself!

> "This activity was a success with the children especially since it was an outdoor activity. We reformed the activity into a type of a treasure hunt finding items from our environment, tying them on the sticks and then placing them in our treasure chest. We saved these 'treasures' to share with Zogg."
>
> Antria Stavrou, To Proto Vima Nursery School, Cyprus

A project funded by the European Union and led in England by CDEC.

5. Gifts from the sea

Using the sea as a stimulus, this activity gives you free reign to follow the interests and abilities of you and your children in an exploration of the importance of the marine environment, and how we can look after it. Pick simpler elements of the activity for younger children in the 5–8 age range.

Subject/Curriculum links
It could be an art project, a history lesson, or used to learn about geography and ecology. The world's your oyster!

Global Learning Aims include
Children understand that there are many different environments on earth and we rely on and use lots of natural resources from them, and we need to look after them.

Personal Learning Goal
The self–directed and discovery nature of this activity helps children with self-awareness, managing feelings, empathy and social skills.

Starter activity

Set the scene by playing a CD of sounds of the sea – waves and seagulls etc. Ask the children what feelings and associations they have in relation to the sea. Responses in Bulgaria where this activity was developed were varied: recreation, fish, mermaid, seashell, mussels, whale, treasure, pirate, Nemo, salty, algae and others. Write all these things up.

Display some resources that you have collected related to the sea –children can explore the different textures, types, colours and smells of items from the sea.

Main learning activity

From the original words children came up with, use open questions and Sustained Shared Thinking to take some aspects of the discussion further. What plants and animals from the sea do they know about? Emphasise the wealth of flora and fauna of the sea, and how much of it is used in our everyday life (fish for food; as a natural resource e.g. salt; seaweed, beautiful landscapes such as coral; precious items such as pearls).

As well as the living things in the sea, talk about the many people whose livelihoods depend on the sea. Look at pictures of people whose occupations are associated with the sea- fishermen, pearl hunters, divers, sailors, keepers of the lighthouses, tourist guides, scientists. On the map of the world give some examples of where each of these roles take place and what the job might be like.

Another topic to explore is "travel by sea": On the world map look at the seas and oceans on which ships carry cargo around the world – you could show how canals like the Suez or Panama canals have shortened huge journeys, or look at famous sea journeys in history and plot those. You could also talk about natural journeys within the sea – find pictures of shoals of fish that sometimes travel thousands of miles to spawn in warm water and then go back again.

It is important to look at the threats to this amazing environment. Focus the discussion on threats to the richness of the sea and how we can support its conservation. This could involve some research done in small groups – each looking at a different aspect. They might look at the threat of climate change (warming and increased acidity due to greater levels of carbon dioxide killing coral for example, or thinning ice in the arctic ocean making life difficult for polar bears); or pollution (e.g. fish and other sea dwellers swallowing plastic and starving, or oil pollution damaging seabirds).

Encourage each group to find things that we can do to protect the sea and share this with the whole class. Conclude that our sea gives us many things, but we have to be responsible and look after it to preserve them for the future.

  A project funded by the European Union and led in England by CDEC.

To finish off…

The final phase of the lesson involves making something precious on a sea theme. Children could work individually or in groups, taking any item that interests them. In Bulgaria where this was trialled one group made a seabed of sand and shells, others painted, cut out or coloured various sea creatures, the rest made accessories of 'pearls' and other sea materials. It could be a whole class project culminating in large display of the ocean, and the people and things that depend on it.

Resources you will need

- Thread
- Coloured paper
- Sand, seashells, dried seaweed – any items from the sea.
- Water-colours
- Plastic plates
- Glue
- Scissors
- CD with a recording of sea sounds
- Map of the world
- Images of shoals of fish

Additional activities you may want to try

This topic of interaction with nature can also be developed for other environments and ecosystems – rainforests for example, or mountain ranges.

> "Discussing the threats to the sea the children realized that each one of us can make an effort to protect it. One of the children said that someday if she meets a golden fish that grants wishes, her wish would be for the sea to be always clean, and that there should be a lot of fish and plants. I led the conversation in the direction whether we need a golden fish to make this happen or can we start to make a difference ourselves if we make some effort? I asked them how each of us can protect the sea and got some very interesting answers: Do not throw waste (plastic bags, food, etc.), for example, or go fishing only where authorized."
>
> Lidia Tseneva, Zdravets Kindergarten, Ihtiman, Bulgaria

6. Zogg's spaceship

This is an active game which can be played indoors or outdoors, for a minimum of 12 children. Children travel round the universe in improvised spaceships before having to negotiate what objects they can take with them on their journey – leading to an introduction of the concept of sustainability and the difference between needs and wants.

Subject/Curriculum links
Teachers have used the main activity as part of a PE lesson, and it also supports listening and team working skills.

Global Learning Aims include
Children will begin to explore concern for, empathy with and sensitivity to others, locally and globally. This activity will help them share and discuss their ideas with others and justify their opinions.

Personal Learning Goal
By setting goals with achievable steps and discussing priorities, this activity builds confidence in social skills and motivation.

Starter activity

Ask children whether they remember Zogg's travel in his spaceship – you may need to remind children of the story or read "Meet Zogg". If you did the "Journey with Zogg" activity from this handbook allow time for children to refresh their memories of their journey. Ask the children whether they are ready to start a journey again. If it is the first time encourage children to try to travel just like Zogg did and explain how to use the materials available – material/sheets, hoops etc. which will enable them to build a spaceship around their team. The construction must somehow connect the team as if travelling in one vehicle, even if it just means holding on to each other, or holding on to the same sheet for example.

Prepare six (depending on numbers) "space ships". Ask children to get into teams of equal numbers and to choose a first leader. Agree with children where the space base is and the whistle signal that tells them to come back to base. Put some music on. Allow the children time to travel moving around at different speeds, reminding them to make sure everyone in the spaceship is safe. Allow time for turn-taking so that everyone in the team has the opportunity to try being a leader – you could pause the music to indicate time to swap. Depending on the ability and physical confidence of the children, you could also suggest that the leader initiates different ways of moving, and the team or crew copies – different speeds, low to the ground bumpily as they enter the atmosphere etc. – all the time making sure the whole team is together and safe.

Main learning activity

Blow the whistle to call all the spaceships back to base and ask the children to get out of their ships and sit in a circle. Tell the teams that they are going to travel to another planet so they need to think what objects/things they would like to take with them and why. Children can draw the object, write its name or say it (depending on learners' age and abilities). Pretend to pack your objects into your ships, and pretend to get dressed into astro suits and board the spaceship. Blow the whistle to signal the start. After some time blow the whistle again asking children to come to the base. Tell them that some of the ships have broken down and can't travel anymore but all the passengers need to continue the journey. Reduce the number of spaceships by half . Ask children to make new teams of equal number. Before the new teams get in their spaceships again tell them about a new dilemma. As there is less space in the spaceship teams need to reduce the number of objects they're taking along. Invite children to sit in circles in their new space teams and spread on the floor their pictures, cards or retell what objects they want take with them. Ask children to choose as a team which objects can go with them (they need to reduce them by two objects). Allow time to think and invite arguments and decisions. After the decision is made blow the whistle so that the teams start their journeys again. You can repeat the procedure until each team can only take one or two objects (depending on the number of pupils and teams you started the game with).

  A project funded by the European Union and led in England by CDEC.

To finish off...

Gather back in the circle and ask:

- What they think about the activity? Did they like it or not? Was it easy/difficult/challenging/stressful? Why?

- How did they choose which objects to take?

- What were the most common objects chosen and why?

- How did it feel having to choose between objects and leave some behind?

- What did they think about when making those decisions as a team?

- Which of the objects are their "needs"? How do they differ from "wants"?

- Is it possible to satisfy everyone's needs/wants? Why?

Bring in the idea that when we make decisions about what we want or need, it affects others. If some people take everything they want, there will not be enough for everyone to have everything they need for life. It is important for us, and for world leaders to make decisions that meet everybody's current needs without spoiling the opportunity for future generations to meet their needs. A simpler definition of sustainability is "enough for everyone, forever" which you might like to introduce.

In the end ask everybody – children and supporting adults – to have a quiet moment of reflection on what they learnt today, and ask if anyone has thoughts they want to share.

Additional activities you may want to try

You could use the pictures of the objects children have drawn and do a sorting activity – sorting into hoops representing needs, and wants. There will be some debate – is a favourite teddy bear a need? They may need it to feel safe? Or a non-essential "want"? And a favourite food – food is essential but do we need so much choice?Allow an overlap for objects that the children can't classify. Discuss whether children in all situations have the same needs and wants. What might children in the different places Zogg visits choose to prioritise on a journey? Remember that within countries and continents there is great diversity – some children in your own country will have very little choice, others huge wealth – the same is true in other places.

Resources you will need

- Elastic material or hoops that can be used to improvise Zogg's spaceship

- Whistle

- Music

- Pieces of paper and crayons

- Imagination!

7. Zogg's house

This junk modelling activity starts by uses Zogg's example of re-using junk to make a house, and explores what makes a house a home. The age range 3–8 could all get something out of this activity.

 Subject/Curriculum links
Various uses of this lesson include environmental education, and science – understanding of different materials and their properties.

 Global Learning Aims include
Children get involved in sustainable actions in the classroom and in the home.

 Personal Learning Goal
Thinking both about the environmental impact of resource use, and different types of housing materials encourages a sense of self awareness, motivation, empathy and social skills.

Starter activity

Introduce the theme of using something for a different purpose by playing this game from Cyprus – "The Merry Chestnuts". The children make a circle and join hands. They begin to sing a song that they all know, and the pace of the melody sets the pace of the game. The children each hold a chestnut, or a conker, or a pebble in the right hand, which they pass into the left hand of their neighbour. They have to keep time and look at each other to make it work. The aim is to speed up and up until they dissolve into laughter!

In advance ask the children to bring in materials from home, old shoeboxes, magazines, plastic bottles, boxes etc.

Main learning activity

Read page 4 of "Meet Zogg". Ask children to come up with ideas about how Zogg might have built his house. What would it be like to live in a house made from an old car? How would it be same/different to living in a house? Think about terms such as warm/cold, boring/fun, soft/hard, comfortable/uncomfortable, small/big, cosy/crowded, and clever as it re-uses old already used materials (recycled). Compare it with building a house with bricks, stone, wood etc.

What could they use to build a house for Zogg if he was to visit the classroom? How would they keep the house together?

Move on to building a house or den for Zogg from the materials provided. This can be as ambitions as is appropriate to your setting – you may want to think carefully about the materials used – what will be waterproof? What will be strong? What will keep him warm – or cool? When you have a structure from junk that could accommodate Zogg, begin to talk about what makes a house a home?

Begin by writing up the two words: "House" and "Home". Ask children if a house and a home are the same thing? Is it just a shelter or do you need other things in it to make it a home? How could we make Zogg feel at home?

Ask them to describe and draw their own homes. Introduce photographs of different types of homes in your own country and other countries. Talk about the similarities and differences between the homes of the children.

Encourage the children to think about:

- The materials used to build homes and the reasons for using different materials – the climate, the environment and landscape
- The features (windows, doors, chimneys, stilts, gardens) and their function
- Who might live in it?
- Is it a permanent or mobile home?
- Use the world map to find where the pictures of the homes are.
- Stimulate discussion about the environment and the home – for example would an igloo be built in Cyprus?

  A project funded by the European Union and led in England by CDEC.

Help the children to reflect that everyone lives somewhere, but some people have more comfortable homes than others. Some are made out of other people's junk – which is very creative, but may not be very comfortable. And although having a house to provide safety and shelter is very important, equally important is what happens there – the family or friends living together and cooking, eating, playing, working, having fun together.

To finish off...

When the discussion draws to a close, and Zogg has left, ask the children to clear all the junk materials away. Sort them into different kinds of materials to recycle them appropriately – plastics, cardboard etc. If there are no facilities in school for recycling, take action to campaign to get recycling bins!

Resources you will need

- Materials like old shoeboxes, plastic bottles, magazines, boxes etc.

- Photographs of different types of homes from your own country and around the world. There is a selection of photos of dwellings used with this activity in Bulgaria included here. Supplement them with your own pictures of different types of houses found locally and around the world. Use your imagination to present as wide a variety as possible, and steer clear of stereotypes!

- World map

- Chestnuts, conkers, pebbles

- Drawing materials

Additional activities you may want to try

A visit to a local recycling centre or landfill site would develop the children's appreciation of the processes involved in recycling. Encourage them to take their learning home and encourage their families to recycle more.

> **"Through these activities they learned to love the environment and strive to become environmentally active and literate citizens."**
>
> **Ioanna Papantoniou, Lemesos 8 Primary School, Cyprus**

A project funded by the European Union and led in England by CDEC.

 A project funded by the European Union and led in England by CDEC.

8. Sustainable table

Making the link between locally produced food and delicious traditions, children and their families collaborate to share their favourite traditional dishes – learning about sustainable food choices along the way. With support from their families, even the youngest can join in.

 Subject/Curriculum links
A research project, a cookery activity, a cultural history element and a lesson on sustainability of local and global food.

 Global Learning Aims include
Children communicate how they feel to peers, parents and other adults and clearly express their point of view.

 Personal Learning Goal
Awareness of where our traditional foods come from, and collaborating with families to share this with peers develops self-awareness, empathy, motivation and social skills.

Starter activity

The activity spreads over a week and includes a family research project. It starts children looking at a selection of photographs of children around the world having breakfast (see Activity 7 page 52). Children are asked to pick up a photo and answer questions like:

- What country might this breakfast come from?

- What does it consist of? Does it look tasty?

- What do you know about this country?

- What do you know about what they grow there?

- What is the climate like?

The teacher highlights that the photos present traditional breakfasts, which are based on local food and have been there for centuries. These may be related to what is traditionally grown locally, and recipes and traditions may have been preserved from previous generations. But remember that traditions can adapt and there may be new elements!

Main learning activity

Then the teacher asks the students to talk to their families about "Our most delicious recipe for the family table". The assignment involves several tasks

- Discuss with their family what their most delicious traditional recipe is and its history

- Find out where the ingredients come from

- Cook the dish with a family member and write simple instructions based on what you did

- Draw a picture or take a photograph of the dish and write the recipe on the back of the drawing.

Give the children two weekends to accomplish the assignment together with their parents.

Then they are asked to present their pictures and descriptions and discuss where the food ingredients come from.

After the presentations, explore the benefits of growing your own food, or buying it locally. Make a list of all the benefits of local food – examples might include less energy involved in transporting it; freshly picked; supports local growers; tastes good; cheaper; less packaging.

To finish off...

The children exchange drawings/ recipes and discuss the similarities among them in terms of what local ingredients are used. Then they 'vote' for their favourite local products.

Then think about any ingredients that you can't get locally produced. What would the dish be like without those ingredients? Cocoa in a chocolate cake for example? Illustrate that while there are many environmental and social benefits of buying local, there are also times when it is good to get things from the rest of the world – and if we make careful choices (such as buying Fairtrade products where possible, and not wasting food, and recycling the packaging) this can also make a positive impact.

Resources you will need

- Photos of international local breakfasts (see activity "What's for breakfast today?")

Additional activities you may want to try

Turn this activity into a festive feast! Invite families to bring in their favourite dishes at the end of term to share in a meal together. The children can present what they learned about sustainable choices in buying food. Read "Lily's Picnic" with the children, and discuss the ingredients of a different type of traditional meal!

> **"The children loved the activity as they communicated with their mothers and grandmothers to report and taste traditional cooking recipes, which reflect the eating traditions in our region. The best drawings / recipes were laminated and exhibited in the classroom."**
>
> **Vanya Yankova, Primary School, Kyril I Metodius, Silistra, Bulgaria**

  A project funded by the European Union and led in England by CDEC.

9. Planet earth – learning from Zargot!

Using the excellent example from Zargot, of re-using old materials, this activity involves cooperation to make footballs from old plastic bags – among other things! Suitable for 5 – 8 year olds – or younger children with more help.

Subject/Curriculum links
This is a craft activity with an environmental message.

Global Learning Aims include
Children show a concern for the environment and a willingness to take care of it, and are able to take part in sustainable action in the classroom.

Personal Learning Goal
Cooperating on a shared activity to look after the environment helps with motivation, empathy and social skills.

Starter activity

Prepare children to meet a new friend– or if you already know him well, announce another visit from Zogg! Read the very beginning of "Meet Zogg", focus on the page where the planet Zargot is described as being made from rubbish from other planets. Ask children what Zogg's house is made from (an old car). And his bed (a shoebox). Zargots are very good at reusing things – what things do we throw away and could we use any of them for anything useful?

Main learning activity

Produce your pile of plastic bags (ask colleagues and parents to bring them in in the weeks before so you have plenty). Ask the children what they think we could make out of these. Take suggestions, and then ask Zogg for a suggestion (if you have a puppet). Zogg tells the children to turn to the pages with the football games, and excitedly points at the football! He explains that not all children here on earth (let alone Zargot) have footballs to play with, and some are very creative at making them from cloth, banana leaves, rubber, and plastic bags – hurray!

Look at the instructions for making footballs out of plastic bags. Arrange the children into small groups, and give them each a pile of bags and string. Help them to decide how they will take turns and organise the process of working together to make the balls. And get going! This takes quite a while, and the tighter they can scrunch the paper and tie the bags, the better the ball will be – they may need an adult helper in each group. You may only get to a ball the size of a tennis ball – but you should end up with something you can play with!

Once they have made the balls, allow them time to play catch or football with them for a while. Then ask how it felt to be playing with something they had made themselves, from stuff that should have been thrown away! Ask what might have happened to the plastic bags if they hadn't used them? (litter, swallowed by birds or fish, clogging up drains etc.) and congratulate them (or get Zogg to) on saving the environment!

To finish off...

Make a certificate from Zogg awarding them the status of "honorary Zargot" for their expertise in recycling and present it in class or assembly.

A project funded by the European Union and led in England by CDEC.

Resources you will need

- "Meet Zogg" book and a Zogg puppet
- A large number of used plastic bags
- String
- Instructions for making plastic footballs at http://www.sendacow.org.uk/lessonsfromafrica/resources/plastic-bag-football
- A Zargotian certificate of excellence in recycling!

For additional activity

- Empty plastic bottles, soil and fast-growing seeds such as cress
- Pom-poms and googly eyes to decorate the planting bottles

Additional activities you may want to try

Turn your attention to the plastic bottles – http://www.diyncrafts.com/4870/home/20-fun-creative-crafts-plastic-soda-bottles

An adult will need to cut off the bottom parts and give one to each child. They can decorate it using pom-poms for eyes, and use the top as a nose – the hair will be the plants growing out of the top! Fill it with soil and scatter some fast-growing seeds such as cress, covering with a thin layer of soil.

Ask the children what these seeds will need to be able to grow – water and light once they start to germinate. Each morning when they come in they can look to see if anything has grown – and of course once grown, they can cut and eat the salad!

Find other things that children around the world make out of things thrown away – greenhouses from plastic bottles, toys from wire, ornaments from plastic bags in South Africa – the possibilities are endless and creative.

> "Children enjoyed and learned together at this early age, they are especially sensitive to new friends, even more so those from 'another planet'. They realized that our planet is full of resources and richness, but we have to be responsible and prudent in using them."
>
> Ilyana Markova, Zdravets Kindergarten, Ihtiman, Bulgaria

 A project funded by the European Union and led in England by CDEC.

Global Learning and Special Educational Needs

The World from our Doorstep activities and participatory approach were greeted enthusiastically by educators and teachers working with children with special educational needs and learning disabilities, particularly by partners in Cyprus and Bulgaria. Teachers took the activities and adapted them to their context and the groups of children that they were working with, placing greater emphasis on the personal and social development elements. The project gave teachers the opportunity to experiment with more participatory approaches, created space for reflection and enabled children to develop their sense of identity and "have a voice". By using World from our Doorstep materials they were surprised at the knowledge and experience some of their students had about the world, which they would never have known without the stimulus of the project. The section below briefly outlines how this worked in Cyprus and Bulgaria.

Case Study 1 - Agios Spyridonas - Special School Larnaka, Cyprus

About the school: The main purpose of Agios Spyridonas is to provide education to children with special needs and learning disabilities in the city and the surrounding district of Larnaka. The school targets not only the spiritual and social side of the students but the mental and physical health of each student individually. It aims to create a pleasant environment in which all children feel happy and secure. The school management model is participatory. The objectives emerge through discussion and consensus. Changes and improvements are decided collectively and collaboratively.

The education of the school aims to offer systematic stability, it recognises and respects the independence, autonomy and individuality of each student and tries to help them within their capabilities:

- To develop and utilise all psychosomatic forces to the highest possible degree

- To become autonomous, comprehensive and useful members of society

- To learn how to acquire knowledge, how to put into practice what they learn, how to coexist, cooperate with others and how to live a full life in the wider community

Why we wanted to be involved in Global Education

Global Education is an important learning method for Special Education Needs schools. Our philosophy is to teach the children to feel they are part of the wider world of everyone, starting out in circles: a small circle which is their own personal space which is part of a bigger circle of their community, which is then part of a bigger circle of their country, their region, the world, the universe. This approach helps children understand that they don't function as separate entities but are part of a whole. The activities and learning methods in the World from our Doorstep are exactly the values and attitudes that we wish to use to help us communicate to our students. Global Education helps the students expand their horizons and understand their place in the world and the interconnectedness that they are part of.

What we did: Teachers from Agios Spyridonas have described the activities they did with children, inspired by the World from our Doorstep resources.

Aboard the spaceship with Zogg

"We viewed on YouTube videos of our solar system so the children could come into contact with the planets and realize that earth is also a planet, then we read the 'Meet Zogg' storybook. Following that we had a discussion with the children about inviting Zogg the alien to our area so we could meet him. Here we facilitated a discussion about where in Cyprus we could take him to visit and the children answered with places they are familiar with and have already visited like: the zoo, the salt lake to see the flamingos, to Platres to see the mountains, the snow, the beach etc. After that we discussed what we would offer him to eat (traditional food) and the children answered kebab, sheftalia, vine leaves and so on. We then discussed what games we would play with him (traditional games) e.g. hide and seek, handkerchief etc."

To a different place with Zogg

"We introduced the idea of Zogg coming to visit our class, then created a dialogue with the children about which

A project funded by the European Union and led in England by CDEC.

countries we could take Zogg to visit. This was a way to encourage children who come from other countries to talk about their countries and bring us some more information. Next we did a presentation with the main attractions of each country (on the interactive whiteboard). We focused mainly on the countries that the children have already visited."

Food from around the world

"To start with we asked the children whether they had tasted dishes from other countries and what these were. Following on from this children brought from home various recipes or homemade dishes from other countries. Through the Health Education lesson the children chose which dishes from other countries they wanted to cook and they cooked a meal. We then compared the dishes from other countries with Cypriot dishes and discussed similarities and differences. Finally, we created our own cookbook with recipes from around the world."

The country that I want to travel to

"The children were invited into a circle to which the 'globe ball' was introduced. Each child threw the ball to the other and said which country they would like to travel to. Each time a child said the country of their choice, we located the country on the world map and the globe ball. We observed the size of each country in comparison to Cyprus and the distance we needed to travel to get there, then talked about the means of transport needed to arrive at our destination. A corner of the room was transformed into a 'Travel Agency' where tickets were issued to each child for the country of their choice."

Travel agency

"The classroom was transformed into a travel agency and the teacher was the travel agent. The children held their tickets. The travel agent gave the children various tourist brochures and informative booklets. The children were asked each in turn to find the country that was written on their ticket. We read information about each of the countries and looked at the pictures. We saw how much money was required for us to travel to this country. Each child found different pictures from the country that they were going to visit with their ticket, on the internet. From this we made a booklet with the title: 'The countries that the children of our class will be travelling to'. In the booklet we are placing all of the pictures that the children found on the internet."

Exploring with Zogg

"This activity involved describing visiting two different scenarios with Zogg: a visit to a clean park with games, trees, and recycling bins; and in contrast a visit to an abandoned park filled with rubbish. The children were asked to locate the differences and similarities and record their conclusions. Questions were raised such as which park they would prefer to be in and what could they do to change the second park. The children then 'adopted' the abandoned park and took care of it until it was clean. We created a book of drawings done by the children of the clean park to give as a present to Zogg to take back to his planet."

Reflections from Agios Spyridonas

"Participating in the project has been an eye-opening experience for us as educators. Through the activities we have been surprised at the knowledge and understanding some of the students have shared with us and we would never have known that they had this knowledge had it not been for the type of activities which offers them an outlet to express this. The project strengthened our school and us as educators. It gave us an insight into other countries and how their Special Education Schools work as well and we were able to exchange knowledge and experiences. By experiencing these activities and methods the children learnt important life skills which will stay with them for their whole lives and assist them in adjusting to everyday life. The philosophy of the project was the same as the philosophy of the school, the learning methods were practical and easy for the students to participate in.

There is no structure or method or guidelines on global education in Cyprus so educators are left to their own devices and have to think of ideas and search for materials by themselves which is very difficult. World from our Doorstep offered the materials, activities and guidelines for us to use and adapt, this is something that as a school and as educators we wanted and needed to have access to. In Cyprus we have the issue of social exclusion of Special Needs students from the rest of the students. By using the same materials, training and characters like Zogg, both SEN and non-SEN children have a common meeting ground and understanding of the world regardless of their ability."

Teachers from Agios Spyridonos participating in World from our Doorstep

George Leontiou, Athina Georgiou, Yiota Papastavrou, Eleni Apostolou, Christina Christodoulou.

  A project funded by the European Union and led in England by CDEC.

Case Study 2 - First Special School - Prof. dps Georgi Angushev, So a, Bulgaria.

About the school

First Special School Prof. dps Georgi Angushev in Sofia was established in 1962 aiming at students who cannot get their education in schools of general education. During the years the school has gone through a lot of reforms and innovations and currently there are 150 students in the school with a range of educational needs or learning disability. The school has established a specialist a team to support and evaluate each child's learning. The team includes teachers, specialists/speech therapist, psychologist, staff with child protection responsibilities and parents. At the beginning of each school year the team prepares an individual programme to support the education and development of each child and during the school year monitors their development. At the end of term and the school year this is used to assess progress and achievements. During the past 2 years global education topics have been included in the different elements of individual programmes for training and development.

Why we wanted to be involved in Global Education

"Students with special education needs are part of the globalized world. They are active participants in it. It is really challenging for us to include global education topics in the individual programmes for our students. This is a great challenge to the team but represents a step change in the development of new educational methods, aimed at

children with disabilities. Through the World from Our Doorstep project we have had the opportunity to work with children, becoming familiar with new methods and concepts, connected to global education. The project provided the opportunity for students to think ahead and to see circumstances and issues within the complexity of a global context. Students have been motivated to reflect and think about their identity and way of life, and to take responsibility. Teachers have been able to grow familiar with and start implementing activities developing global education values, which helps students to be responsible as citizens not only on a personal level, but also on a local and global level."

Teachers reflected on how the project activities enable students with special education needs to feel equal with the other people in the globalised world as well as a range of issues such as environmental sustainability, healthy food, sport and tourism. Through the project activities students developed communication, team work and decision making skills. Teachers also described how the project approaches promoted equality and being responsible for our world, as well as a realisation of responsibilities, obligations and rights.

What we did

Teachers selected and adapted activities keeping in mind the abilities of the students they were working with in small groups (up to 5 children). This was to ensure the quality of the activity and participation of the children. Natural materials (clay and sand), fruits, vegetables, etc. were commonly used as a stimulus for the activities. Teachers highlighted the importance of communication with parents too: "We regularly communicate with the parents as we provide feedback about how their children were involved in global education lessons."

One activity developed and adapted by the teachers of Prof. dps Georgi Angushev is outlined here:

It is not fair!

Learning aims: To explore ideas of justice, equality and honesty in students

Description: "The teacher prepared a bowl with fruits (bananas, apples) and

and cake. The children sat in a circle and in front of each child was put a different product. Some children were given all the products. We observed the reaction of students. Some of them were happy, but some of them were angry. The teacher asked questions: Were the products correctly distributed among children? Why did some of them have more and others less? Was it fair? Why did this happen? How could we avoid it if we do not like this distribution? The children were unanimous that all of them should have had an equal number of products. We asked the children to distribute the products among each other. We conducted a discussion that when somebody acts unfairly it might hurt his relatives, his family and as a summary – it might cause poverty of people in some states. We explored the idea of sharing toys or treats with their friends, and how they felt if they got nothing when somebody else got something. Making wider connections through this process of realisation and perception was very important. The children usually 'recognised' themselves in the specific situation described, so we encouraged them to make the link from the personal (me, my family, my world) to wider connections (their community, society, and finally thinking globally).

At the end of the game the children summarised the conclusion that each one of us should be honest and fair."

Resources: Fruits – apples and bananas, cake

 A project funded by the European Union and led in England by CDEC.

Working with local producers and craftspeople

World from our Doorstep encouraged educators to engage with local craftspeople and artisans to make the themes of fairness and sustainability real and meaningful from a very local perspective. This was achieved through local producers visiting schools and creating "day in the life" stories about their lives and work, to show diversity and connect the local to the global; celebrating local and fair produce with a Fairtrade producer from Belize visiting Cumbria in March 2015 and in family workshops exploring the journeys that food and craft products take from raw material to final product. Many "day in the life" stories can be found on the project website: www.worldfromourdoorstep.com

This section highlights some activities from Bulgaria which particularly draw on the input and expertise of local producers.

Story 1: Thea's favourite treats - activity with a visit from a local honey producer

Introduction

This activity demonstrated the role of bees in nature and explained some reasons for the reduction in bee populations as well as ways to prevent their extinction. It provided an opportunity to learn about the variety of bee products. The children entered into the "role" of bees from the hive and felt like part of a larger community. They gained awareness of the role of bees in agriculture, and that without them the natural cycle and the world around us would not be sustainable.

The original activity took place with a local honey producer in Bulgaria in October 2014, when the honey harvest was being collected. He provided honey at the beginning of the lesson, so the children were able to try it. The activity started with a discussion about how much Thea would enjoy eating honey! We asked the children what they thought: did she prefer chocolate to honey? What was needed in order to produce chocolate and what to produce honey? During the lesson as a background the sound of buzzing bees was played. The aim was for the children to share what they felt as if they were on a summer walk in the woods.

The lesson takes place in three parts:

Starter activity

This introduced the idea that Thea, like any other bear, likes to eat honey and asked the children whether they knew where honey comes from. At this point the local producer explained simply how a bee's body is structured and its method of collecting pollen, production and storage of nectar, honeycombs, bee-keeping, and care for the beekeeper hives.

Main learning activity:

a. What we know about the bees?

During this session using the expertise of the beekeeper we discussed: What gives us honey and why we eat it? Whether it is difficult to raise bees and how much the labour of the beekeeper costs? Should honey be Fairtrade? Why bees are decreasing every year and some species are threatened with extinction? What would be the consequences of the disappearance of bees? What can all of us do to save the bees?

An interesting moment of the lesson was to get children to make "the sweet path of Thea". The students were divided into two teams. The children had to show how many stages there are in the production of honey and chocolate. Every child in the team presented an individual step of the process. All the children were involved by adding their own opinion to the stories of their classmates. NB this required reading "Thea Discovers Chocolate" so children had a clear introduction to how chocolate is made. You will find a short animated film based on a "Day in the Life of a Honey Maker" at www.worldfromourdoorstep.com, and a honey maker is also one of the characters in "Lily's Picnic".

b. Visit to an apiary

An extension of this activity was to visit a bee farm (apiary). In this context children saw "live" the habitat of bees, they looked at the honeycomb and had the opportunity to take out honey using a special machine "a honey extractor".

To finish off...

The activity expanded and enriched the knowledge of the children about the long production "path" for both honey and chocolate. We reflected with the children on the basic steps covered in order for honey or chocolate to reach our table (again drawing on the experience of the beekeeper). This activity elaborated on the "Thea Discovers Chocolate" story.

A project funded by the European Union and led in England by CDEC.

Using the advice and input of the beekeeper ideas such as finding out where to buy local honey, whether their local shops sell Fairtrade honey and ideas towards protecting the natural resources/habitat for bees were discussed

Resources you will needed

Paper model of the basic parts of a bee – that could be assembled/disassembled, "Thea Discovers Chocolate" and "Lily's Picnic" story books; empty frame of a beehive; jar of honey; bee propolis (bee 'glue' that they collect from tree buds/sap etc.); wax candle; photos of beehives; soundtrack of buzzing bees

> **"Children are very entertained during this lesson. During the game 'Thea's Favourite Treats' each child is trying to show how important every stage of production of the chocolate and honey is. The fact that they visit and see 'live' how the bee farm works, how to take out honey, how the bees are being fed, etc. was an invaluable lesson for them. The local manufacturer was also excited about being involved and expressed the wish for more such joint lessons."**
>
> Vera Koleva , Dimtcho Debelyanov School, Ihtiman, Bulgaria

Story 2: Appreciate the labour of others

Introduction

This activity aimed to develop the awareness of children in relation to local production and Fairtrade, building their understanding of the differences in local production and Fairtrade. It also familiarised the children with the production process in different types of farms.

Starter activity

The lesson took place outdoors. In Bulgaria, where this activity was developed, the children visited the local producers from the region of Ihtiman. The teacher began with a discussion about "Thea Discovers Chocolate" – it was necessary to read this to the class The story was used to explore children's perceptions of Fairtrade, again through class discussion.

Main learning activity

The lesson included visits to various local producers (in the UK this might include local farms; or craftspeople/artisans producing local goods). In Bulgaria the children visited a vegetable garden and workshop for clothing production. In both places manufacturers acquainted children with the difficulties and challenges in their activities, followed by a discussion which used the following questions: How and why is the work of these local producers important? How does this fit with buying goods produced elsewhere? Is their production Fairtrade? Are the manufacturers familiar with products of that mark? How does local production influence the local community and economy? Does the profit that the manufacturer gets help social, environmental or other causes? How does the concept of Fairtrade apply to local producers – do they regard themselves as working in a fair way?

To finish off...

Discussion on the visit stimulated different views on the significance of local production (its advantages, any disadvantages, benefits to the local economy/environment/food miles etc.) and brought direct comparison/thought to the idea of Fairtrade (and how it is applied in very different global settings but with similar attention to the social and environmental impact of food production).

Vera Koleva, Anna Kolarova – Teachers, Dimtcho DebelyanovSchool, Ihtiman, Bulgaria – teachers

A project funded by the European Union and led in England by CDEC.

Story 3: The Martenitsa maker

Introduction

This activity aimed to develop the sense of interconnectedness and friendship between the children from the countries participating in the project. By using the traditional martenitsa approach from Bulgaria the lesson also contributed to developing understanding and appreciation of the local crafstpeople work.

Starter activity

To introduce the topic and the craftsperson, read the story 'A Day in the Life of a Martenitsa Maker' from the project web site (www.worldfromourdoorstep.com/images/pdf/DayInLife/Martenitsa.pdf).

Main learning activity

STEP 1

STEP 2

Tell the children that they are going to handmake martenitsa together with the local martenitsa maker and should follow her professional instructions. At the same time as the martenitsa itself is 'woven' by white and red yarn, the children are encouraged to work in pairs in order to help each other. To start with they should twist the red and white threads together.

The local craftsperson uses dyed original wool to prepare the 'blossom' of the martenitsa. She combines three colours of wool to form the upper part of the martenitsa. To tighten the blossom to the twisted threads use a wooden button.

STEP 3

STEP 4

Children follow this approach shaping the 'blossom' by using their fingers to make it softer. Then by helping each other they fasten the coloured yarn blossom to the martenitsa threads and tighten them with the button.

It takes quite a while until each pair of pupils finishes one handmade martenitsa. Then the process is repeated to produce the second martenitsa so that both participants have one. They can wear them around their wrist. According to traditional you should wear it until you see the first stork as a sign of the coming spring.

The martenitsa in the pictures were handmade by the pupils from two classes and their teachers Stefka Stoyanova and Milena Marinova, from N.Yonkov Vaptsarov Elementary School. They were made as gifts to other children from Poland, Cyprus and Britain.

A project funded by the European Union and led in England by CDEC.

THE FINAL PRODUCT

THE EXCHANGE

A project funded by the European Union and led in England by CDEC.

Acknowledgements

big "thank you" to the teachers, practitioners and education professionals involved in the development of the activities in e handbook. They enthusiastically took up the ideas, approaches and resources of World from our Doorstep – without them ere would be no handbook!

Cyprus

orge Leondiou, Agios Spyridonas Special School
hina Georgiou, Agios Spyridonas Special School
ota Papastavrou, Agios Spyridonas Special School
eni Apostolou, Agios Spyridonas Special School
ristina Christodoulou, Agios Spyridonas Special School
nna Evdokiou, Parekklisias Primary school
tychia Nikolaou, Kolossiou 1 Public Nursery school
elina Karayianni, Kolossiou 1 Public Nursery school
ene Theofanous Rousia , Kolossiou 1 Public Nursery school
anna Papantoniou, Lemesos 8 Primary school
eda Iacovidou – Ailianou, Lemesos 8 Primary school
ena Aristidou, Lemesos 8 Primary school
ersa Petrou, Lemesos 8 Primary school
antelitsa Zeniou , Lemesos 8 Primary school
aria Loizou, Pissouriou Primary School
rodroma Kleanthous, Geroskipou 2 Public Nursery School
ntria Stavrou, To Proto Vima Nursery School
iza Vasou, To Proto Vima Nursery School
Panayiota Christoforou, To Proto Vima Nursery School
eorgia Michael, Pefkios Georgiadis Primary School
rene Demosthenous, Chryseleousa Primary School
Charis Theocharous, Chryseleousa Primary School
Nicoleta Palate , To Prasino Feggari Nursery School
Marilena Polykarpou, To Prasino Feggari Nursery School
Niovi Michael, Agiou Dimitriou Primary School
Rodoula Pavlidou Karapataki , Aglantzia 6 Public Nursery School
Kalliopi Fountouli, Faneromenis Public Nursery School
Marilena Stylianou, Pefkios Georgiadis Primary School
Chrystalla Nicolaou, Tseriou Public Nursery School
Charoulla Petrokosta, Anthoupolis Primary School
Sophia Pantziarou Kontaxi, Ypsona 1 Primary School
Agni Exadaktylou, Pera Choriou Nisou 1 Primary School
Anna Solomou Konstantinidou, Daliou 3 Primary School
Despo Soteriou, Makedonitissas 2 Primary School
Stathis Vassilas, Kalogera Primary School
Katerina Charalambous, Sotiros Public Nursery School
Maria Charalambous Pishia, Sotiros Public Nursery School
Panayiota Papaioannou, Dromolaxias 1 Primary School
Georgia Hadjipanayiotou, Lemesou 9 – Kapsalou Primary School
Michalis Vasiliou , Kato Polemidion 2 – Agiou Georgiou Primary School
Nikolaou A. Nikolaou, Germasogeias 2 Primary School
Ρεβέκκα Μανιώρη , Pafou 9 – Petrideio Public Nursery School
Clare Crouch, Little Stars montessori
Monika Fillaova, Little Stars montessori
Emma Howard, Little Gems montessori
Carola Lang Howard, Little Gems montessori
Elena Savva, Little Gems montessori
Charlotte Hylands, Little Gems montessori
Alexia Ketonis , Highgate Private School
Styliana Odysseos, Highgate Private School
Leigh Fox, Highgate Private School
Christina Iosifidou, Agion Anargyron Public Nursery School
Antri Nicolettou, Lemsou 20–Agiou Panteleimona Public Nursery School

In Poland

Karolina Szczepańska, preschool no.5, Wołomin
Katarzyna Sajkowska
Joanna Pruszyńska, preschool no.174, Warsaw
Katarzyna Anyszewska, preschool teacher, Warsaw.
Irena Majchrzak

In Bulgaria

Dimitar Tsvetanov, 1st Special School, Prof. dps Georgi Angushev, 1st Special School, Sofia
Latinka Kovatcheva, 1st Special School, Prof. dps Georgi Angushev, 1st Special School, Sofia
Adriana Dobreva, Primary school Hristo Botev, Alfatar
Nikolinka Zlateva, Primary school Hristo Botev, Alfatar
Vanya Yankova, Primary school Kyril I Metodius, Silistra
Ilyana Markova, Kindergarten Zdravets, Ihtiman
Dilka Filipova, Kindergarten Zdravets, Ihtiman
Lidia Tseneva, Kindergarten Zdravets, Ihtiman
Stilka Gerinska, Kindergarten Zdarvets, Ihtiman
Mariana Gagova, Primary school Otets Paisii, Silistra
Givka Gekova, Primary school Otets Paisii, Silistra
Vera Koleva, School Dimtcho Debelyanov, Ihtiman
Anna Kolarova, School Dimtcho Debelyanov, Ihtiman
Stefka Stoyanova, School N.Yonkov Vaptsarov
Milena Marinova, School N.Yonkov Vaptsarov

In the UK

Helen Evans and Sarah Edmondson, Holy Family Catholic Primary School, Barrow-in-Furness
Lisa Fell, Newton Primary School, Newton-in-Furness
Zoe Brettle, Pennybridge Nursery, Greenodd
Naomi Slater, Sacred Heart Catholic Primary School, Barrow-in-Furness
Angela Pope, St Columba's Catholic Primary School, Barrow-in-Furness
Cath Smethurst and Kim Allder, St Oswald's CE Primary School, Burneside
Amy Bates, St Pius X Catholic Primary School, Barrow-in-Furness
Anne Emms, Church Walk CE Primary School, Ulverston
Lucy Holland, Inglewood Community Nursery and Infant School, Carlisle
Carmen Armstrong, Ivegill Nursery, Ivegill, Carlisle
Leanne Storey, Kingmoor Nursery and Infant School, Carlisle
Kelly Kavanagh, Raughton Head CE Primary School, Dalston
Diane Rothery, Upperby Primary School, Carlisle
Val Gillespie, Wiggonby CE Primary School, Wiggonby

Special Thanks

Erika Demetriou , European and International Affairs Officer – Ministry of Education and Culture
Aravella Zachariou, Coordinator of Environmental Education and Sustainable Development Department
Yiola Erodotou, Center for Environmental Education Athalassa (Pedagogical Institute)
Nicolaos A. Nicolaou, Center for Environmental Education Athalassa (Pedagogical Institute)
Koula Michael, Center for Environmental Education Akrotiri (Pedagogical Institute)
Sofi Kamenou, Center for Environmental Education Akrotiri (Pedagogical Institute)

A project funded by the European Union and led in England by CDEC.